Holywood

Its Cinema & Other Memories

Ken Russell

Acknowledgements

My thanks to the following for their generous help:

The *County Down Spectator* for permission to use various photographs, advertisements and articles of news

Paul Malone for copies of cinema programmes

Colin Steele for photographs of Holywood Cinema

The information within this book has been presented as accurately as possible; however, the author apologises for any inaccuracies or errors that may appear within.

Contents

INTRODUCTION

The idea of this book is to very briefly recapture and remember a place that was once a part of the fabric of Holywood; a place where Holywood people could go to relax for a few hours; a time when Holywood had its very own cinema – originally there were two. Sadly, only memories of it now remain; the cinema has been demolished, making way for a newer, more modern building. These are some of my memories of the last surviving cinema in Holywood from schooldays until around the 1970s, both as a customer and as an employee working there. As well as this, we will also have a brief look at other snippets of information relevant to the town over the years, both recent and historic.

Vast changes have taken place since the first ever movies arrived to thrill audiences throughout the world. These were silent black-and-white films with flickering pictures taken with a hand-cranked camera, and were often accompanied by someone playing a piano in the cinema to add to the atmosphere. Captions that audiences could read were added to the film, and the first films produced were quite short. Eventually film cameras and projectors became more advanced as more money was ploughed into new technology in the film industry, and the variety and quality of films continued to improve. Talking movies came along; the first film being *The Jazz Singer* in 1927, which amazed everyone. Cinemas themselves continued to improve with advanced sound systems, bigger screens, better seating, etc. In some cinemas, during intervals or before shows started, the wonderful Wurlitzer organ took over from the piano and played a nonstop melody of modern tunes to keep the audience entertained. There has been a great change from some of the old cinemas nicknamed 'the fleapit', with their very basic comfort, to the modern multi-screen surround-sound cinemas that have now arrived. Over the years, there have been various film studios throughout the British Isles, Ireland and the USA that have made and produced some wonderful films, such as Elstree, Ardmore in Ireland, MGM, Pinewood, Shepperton, Bray, Twickenham, the Rank Organization,

Warner Bros., Metro-Goldwyn-Mayer, Columbia, Paramount, 20th Century Fox, RKO Radio Pictures, Republic Productions, United Artists, and so on. Films were shown worldwide. Almost everyone loved the American films; they appeared more glamorous and exciting, but this was possibly because they commanded a larger production budget.

Going to the cinema was a treat for young and old, and for years in Holywood's cinemas thousands of people were entertained with a large choice of films ranging from sad to romantic, comedy, horror, comedy, murder mystery, travel, war, etc. As the films changed twice a week, if you had the money you could watch a different film every few nights; for the film fanatic this was heaven. In the cinema's heyday, it was common for there to be queues on Holywood's High Street every evening as people jostled to get into the cinema before the show started and get a seat; otherwise it meant having to stand at the rear of the cinema, if you got in at all. Going to the cinema was not just about watching the film – it was the whole experience: the waiting, the excitement, the expectation.

Some forms of entertainment, in particular television, were not as common as they are today – in fact one can remember how when young we had to make a lot of our own entertainment, playing games such as cowboys and Indians around our local haunts, or marbles or conkers. Many a day was spent searching around the trees of Holywood for the biggest, brightest conkers. So the local cinema was an escape to the world of adventure, magic and imagination, and, without it, to some there would have been a void in our years of growing up. It meant a chance to look out into the world of both make-believe and fact, without actually entering it.

When going to the movies some people called the cinema by a different name, for example the pictures, the movies, flix, the fleapit, movie theatre, movie house, multiplex or picture house.

Holywood's first original cinema was situated at the corner of Shore Street and Marine Parade, opposite what eventually became the Star and Garter pub. The pub was knocked down to facilitate the new bypass. This cinema was called the Maypole Cinema, and it opened at a time when Holywood needed some form of entertainment for visitors as well as locals; cinemas were starting to appear and become

2

popular throughout Northern Ireland. The cinema opened around 1915; it had a proscenium that was 18 feet and also a balcony and it used a British Thomson-Houston sound system. The building it was located within had been used at different times as assembly rooms and a venue for council meetings. It had also been used and was very popular as public baths, drawing people from nearby Belfast, as in those days Holywood was classed as a holiday resort. A warm salt water bath cost 1s, a tepid shower bath 4d and a cold shower bath 3d. Before the railway line extended to Bangor, Holywood had become a type of health spa with its seaside and fresh country air; somewhere regarded as healthy to visit and live in. Indeed, in February 1934 at a meeting of the local council the shortage and need for accommodation for visitors was discussed; it was decided that the town clerk would put up a notice asking for names of local people willing to board visitors during the summer months.

The Maypole Cinema had a continuous show from 6.30pm daily with matinees on a Saturday. Prices for admission to the cinema ranged from 6d to 1s for a seat, and children accompanied by an adult got in for half price. They showed, as with other cinemas of the time, a variety of films to suit all tastes.

The cinema was popular and drew quite a large audience from Holywood and beyond, and for a period of time had the monopoly in Holywood. The Maypole Cinema was unfortunately destroyed by fire in the 1940s, but by that time Holywood had another, newer cinema. The company name 'Holywood Maypole Cinema' remained live until 1960 when it was classed by the Register of Companies for Northern Ireland as dissolved.

Maypole Cinema

HOLYWOOD **PHONE 285**

	PROGRAMME FOR OCTOBER, 1937	
FRIDAY OCTOBER 1st TWO DAYS	**WINDBAG THE SAILOR** also "THE THREE STOOGES"	WILL HAY
MONDAY OCTOBER 4th TWO DAYS	**FLORIDA SPECIAL** JIMMY ALLAN in "SKY PARADE"	JACK OAKIE SALLY EILERS KENT TAYLOR
WEDNESDAY OCTOBER 6th TWO DAYS	**BEN HUR**	RAMON NOVARRO CARMEL MYERS MAY M'AVOY
FRIDAY OCTOBER 8th TWO DAYS	**TARZAN ESCAPES**	JOHNNY WEISSMULLER MAUREEN O'SULLIVAN JOHN BUCKLER BENITA HUME
MONDAY OCTOBER 11th TWO DAYS	**SABOTAGE** also ANDY CLYDE COMEDY	SYLVIA SYDNEY JOHN LODER
WEDNESDAY OCTOBER 13th TWO DAYS	**WOMEN ARE TROUBLE** also "MAN BEHIND THE MASK"	STUART ERWIN PAUL KELLY FLORENCE RICE
FRIDAY OCTOBER 15th TWO DAYS	**RHYTHM ON THE RANGE** BUSTER CRABBE in "NEVADA"	BING CROSBY FRANCES FARMER BOB BURNS
MONDAY OCTOBER 18th TWO DAYS	**POPPY** WILLIAM BOYD in "BAR-20 RIDES AGAIN"	W. C. FIELDS ROCHELLE HUDSON RICHARD CROMWELL
WEDNESDAY OCTOBER 20th TWO DAYS	**CRIME OVER LONDON** also MONTY COLLINS COMEDY	MARGOT GRAHAME PAUL CAVANAGH JOSEPH CAWTHORNE
FRIDAY OCTOBER 22nd TWO DAYS	**YOURS FOR THE ASKING** FRANCES FARMER in "BORDER FLIGHT"	GEORGE RAFT DOLORES C. BARRYMORE IDA LUPINO
MONDAY OCTOBER 25th TWO DAYS	**PALM SPRINGS AFFAIR** also "THE RETURN OF SOPHIE LANG"	FRANCES LANGFORD Sr GUY STANDING ERNEST COSSART
WEDNESDAY OCTOBER 27th TWO DAYS	**LOVE ON THE RUN**	JOAN CRAWFORD CLARKE GABLE FRANCHOT TONE
FRIDAY OCTOBER 29th TWO DAYS	**CHICK** CHARLES STARRETT in "GALLANT DEFENDER"	SYDNEY HOWARD FRED CONYNGHAM ANN DAVIS

There are many younger people, and those who have recently moved to Holywood, who would never have believed that Holywood had at one time two cinemas, and who are quite surprised to learn of their existence. At the time when both cinemas were in operation, if asked which cinema you were going to you would have said either the 'top house' (the new cinema) or the 'bottom house' (the older one), probably because the latter was at the bottom of a small hill.

4

One can see the popularity of cinemas that were operating in 1928 if you look at the number operating in Belfast city (list below); 1940 produced 33 cinemas in Belfast alone.

Alambra
Arcadian
Central Picture Theatre
Classic Cinema
Clonard Picture House
Coliseum
Crumlin Picture House
Diamond Picture House
Duncairn Super Cinema
Gaiety
Imperial Picture House
Kelvin Picture Palace
Lyceum Cinema
Lyric (formerly the Panopticon)
Midland Picture House
New Princess Palace
Picturedrome
Queens Picture and Variety
Royal Cinema
Sandro Cinema
Shankill Picturedrome
The Picture House
West End Picture House
Willowfield Picture House

Holywood Cinema

On 11th December 1933 Holywood Cinema Co. Ltd was formed and registered, the directors being Mr J. Turner and Mr R. Turner. The cinema was started at a time when it was thought that a larger, more modern cinema would be in demand in Holywood, and it certainly was. Eventually, a number of the Turner family became involved in the cinema.

The Holywood New Cinema was built on an excellent central spot, at the junction of Downshire Road and Main Street. This was the site of what was originally Holywood Police Barracks. The cinema was managed by Mrs R. Noble, who also became a director. Cinematic equipment used was made by Western Electric Co. and the sound system was Thomson-Houston. The screen size was 26 feet and the proscenium width was 28 feet. Prices of admission ranged from 3d to 1s.3d. There was seating for 450 people, but even so this was small compared to some of the cinemas in Belfast or the Tonic in Bangor. Staff consisted of the manager, a projectionist, ushers, a secretary, a cashier and cleaners.

In the 1960s and 1970s Mr John Turner was the manager/director, managing what was a fairly busy local entertainment spot. Other popular entertainment in the town at this time included weekly dancing in the Queens Hall and entertainment at the Strathearn Hotel, which drew quite a lot of visitors from Belfast. Mr Turner managed the cinema until its closure. Black-and-white television was around, then colour – an alternative to the cinema – but a lot of people could not afford a television so they rented. Also, people were concerned that if they bought a television set it could break down and cost too much to repair.

Hardly a week went past when, if you had the money, you would eagerly head down to queue at the cinema to see the latest film showing. Unfortunately in those days, perhaps because there were so many cinemas trying to grab custom at a time when television was creeping in, the big well-advertised films (that we would now call blockbuster movies) were not always shown immediately in a cinema the size of Holywood's, which meant a trip to Bangor or Belfast. Holywood Cinema was owned by local people, whilst some others were part of a chain of cinemas throughout the British Isles.

Surrounding towns all had their own cinemas, such as the Regal in Newtownards, the Picture House in Comber, the Cinema in Portaferry, the Regal in Donaghadee and the Tonic in Bangor, although Bangor had more than one cinema. However, there is no place like home, and our own little cinema, although not up to the high standards of some other cinemas (being smaller and having no cafeteria, rising organ or luxury seats) was adequate in providing us with entertainment, without the cost of travel.

Holywood Cinema itself was a commodious red-brick building architecturally built in line with a lot of other cinemas of the period, but to some people it would not have been looked upon as an attractive building. The front entrance of the building, which consisted of three floors, faced the main road. The body of the building stretched along Downshire Road. On the High Street, opposite the cinema, stood Leslie Innis's garage. On the ground level there was the foyer entrance – the entrance itself was not overly impressive but this led into the ticket kiosk, the stalls, and stairs to the balcony and the toilets. In the main auditorium there were more toilets at the rear. Behind the screen in the basement was the boiler to provide heating. The next floor up brought you to the manager's office, and the third floor was where the projection box and balcony were situated, the projection box being slightly higher than the balcony. Adjacent to all three floors was the auditorium. The cinema was one of Holywood's most sizeable buildings at the time, but unfortunately there was no space for parking and those who arrived in cars had to jostle for a space on the High Street or adjoining roads; the majority of patrons, however, were normally within walking distance. A bus stop stood just outside the cinema, making it convenient for some people.

The cinema after closure

At the front of the building, on the High Street, a number of small windows dotted the red brickwork; some of these belonged to the projection room and others were adjacent to the manager's office –

8

these were partially stained and leaded glass; the rest of the windows let light into the toilets and staircases. Originally there was a large vertical sign attached to the corner wall bearing the word 'CINEMA' as well as a large partial glass canopy over the entrance with the word written on its sides, but this was changed in later years to something that resembled a miniature garage forecourt canopy.

The main entrance was through four large, heavy, swinging blue-painted glass doors, and over to the right on the outside wall there were two wood-and-glass frames displaying advertisements for the latest films. These were excellent for advertising what was showing or about to be shown to patrons who were queuing to gain admission. The posters inside the frames were changed weekly when new films arrived. One corner on the front of the building, adjacent to Downshire Road, was turned into a shop selling confectionery, cigarettes, etc. The shop itself was let out for a period before eventually being revamped and combined with the cinema, after which a small glass access window was eventually made through to the cinema foyer so that patrons could purchase sweets, cigarettes, etc. when entering the cinema or in the middle of the show, without leaving the building. Above the front part of the building was a flat roof with a large ventilator fan, built into the wall with pipes running through to the inner roof for ventilation. A wonderful view over Holywood and Belfast Lough could be had from here, as well as a good suntan on a sunny day.

Cinema

An Ariel view of the cinema

Before the decline of the cinema it was not unusual to see queues forming every evening, particularly when there was a popular film showing. Waiting in the queue added to the excitement, and having two films on show meant that even though you might not see the supporting or 'wee' film there was a good chance you would see the entire main feature film or 'big picture'. Most cinemas of today only show the one main feature film so, really, looking back, I would say we got our money's worth.

Queuing was all part of the big build-up in going to the cinema. Looking at the posters would add to the enjoyment, as would observing the different people that you knew or didn't know: families, single people, lovers, children and elderly people. Some people had their favourite film stars, and on every occasion when there was a film showing in which that particular actor/actress starred you could be assured their fans would be there in the queue. You could not help overhearing the different stories, news and personal details as people talked to fill the time whilst waiting. One thing you did hate to hear was someone telling someone else how the film you were about to watch ended, spoiling the plot completely! Some who had bought sweets to eat whilst watching the film ending up munching their way through them whilst waiting, having to stop at the cinema shop on the way in to replenish them. On wet, windy nights, people huddled together in their coats trying to keep warm and breathed a sigh of relief when the queue shuffled forward. Those who were late hoped that there were still vacant seats; otherwise they were left standing outside, exposed to the elements. Unfortunately, we were about to see the reverse happening – queues disappearing along with audiences.

The Downshire Road end of the cinema consisted of a flat bricked wall, with some decorative brick and windows, downspouts and an exit door at the far end. At the front end corner there was for a time a large poster billboard advertising the week's films. When posters were displayed, someone with a large bucket of paste and a brush covered the board with paste before the poster was put up; every so often, however, the old posters had to be removed as they started to peel off because there were so many on top of each other and the wind would blow them down. The board was eventually removed.

At the rear of the cinema there was a small alley leading out onto Downshire Road – this alleyway still exists at the rear of the new building; the other end of it then led into a vacant garden which progressed up the other side of the cinema before arriving at the rear of some buildings, one of which eventually became the Northern Bank.

THE MANAGER

Mr John Turner, a director and owner, eventually took over as the general manager of the Holywood Cinema; he was in charge in the 1960s and 1970s and right through until it closed. He was a very approachable, helpful and courteous person. He had a great interest in and knowledge of horses and horse breeding. At the time a man of middle age, he could usually be seen, if not wearing a suit, donning a tweed coat with a hanky hanging out of the top pocket and grey flannels, parading along the rear of the balcony or stalls checking that everything was in order and noting how many customers were at the show. A trait he had was, when standing with his hand in his pocket, he would turn any coins he had over and over, creating a jingling from his pocket. As with all managers, he was totally responsible for the complete running of the cinema; this included the responsibility for health and safety, making sure staff were trained, ordering films, tickets, organising programmes, dealing with complaints, looking after the intake of cash, staff, cleaners, emergencies, wages, checking light bulbs were working, dealing with drunks, and so on. Another job was looking after the cinema shop, making sure it was fully stocked up and staffed. Complaints from patrons could range from sitting on chewing gum to not being able to see the film because the person in front was too tall, or people wanting their money back because they did not see the whole show, even though they may have arrived late! He would regularly check the ticket kiosk to see how many customers had arrived and make sure that there was enough change.

Halfway up the stairs leading to the balcony was his office, in which his secretary and he worked. As one of Mr Turner's favourite passions was horses, around the walls hung various horse pictures. Soft carpet lined the floor and various cinema literature, rolls of tickets and film posters were sitting around. The furniture consisted of a table, chairs, a filing cabinet and a settee. When you visited his office he could often be found looking through the different film brochures, checking as to what films he was going to order next. Glancing through the brochures supplied by the distributors was fascinating; they gave you a complete insight into the film along with loads of ideas for advertising the film, and this included photographs, posters and merchandise. Although he mainly worked in the cinema at night, he would pop in during the day to sort out paperwork, or to deliver or collect film canisters – these he would collect from the local film distributers. Films he could order were dictated by availability, popularity and cost. He had to consider: is the film popular, is it a new release, what does the audience expect, how much will it cost to rent, and what type of audience would it be suitable for?

Being a director and manager, Mr Turner was always in the cinema each evening to make sure everything ran efficiently and, of course, to keep a check on the financial side of the business. As well as taking an interest in the running of the cinema he also took an interest in his staff, and on many occasions when you would pass him when working there he would stop and ask how you were getting on.

Running a cinema, like with any other business, means having to make enough money to cover all your costs and make a profit. When you consider the price of a ticket, quite a lot of tickets needed to be sold to ensure your expenses were covered. Costs included: film rental; running and replacement of equipment; wages for the staff, projectionist, ushers, cashiers, cleaners and management; mortgage or rent; rates; taxes; heating; electric; advertising; license; and insurance. On top of this, a profit had to be made.

Before the decline of the cinema and television came along queues were quite common at the cinema and often all seats were taken, which meant a good intake of revenue. The type of film could also determine how many patrons attended. However, when television sets, and then videos, became more common, queues at the cinema started to become a thing of the past, resulting in a drastic fall in revenue. At that stage, other ideas to bring in more revenue were tried. In 1958 local cinemas complained about the number of private clubs showing 16mm films; these clubs were allowing non-members to watch films, which meant cinemas were losing potential customers.

THE PROJECTIONIST

Patrick Malone, projectionist

Probably the most important person in the cinema was the projectionist, for without him/her there was no show. Their skills and knowledge kept the film running smoothly and the patrons happy.

The last projectionist to work in the Holywood Cinema was Patrick Malone, a skilled and knowledgeable projectionist. Pat was the cinema's projectionist for many years, right up until it closed. His job consisted of a number of tasks such as:

- [ ] Continuously checking to ensure the projectors were in good order.
- [ ] Receiving and checking films that arrived; making sure they were in good condition.
- [ ] Loading the film onto the projectors.
- [ ] Making sure the film ran smoothly.
- [ ] Changing reels at the appropriate times.
- [ ] Ensuring the sound was correct for the audience.
- [ ] Keeping the film in focus.
- [ ] Keeping the projector light at the correct brightness by adjusting the carbon rods as they burnt down.
- [ ] Checking he had enough carbon rods for the film show.
- [ ] Making sure the curtains and lights worked.
- [ ] Splicing film together if a film broke during the show.
- [ ] Ensuring the film was wound and packed when finished, ready to be sent back to the distributor.

As well as being the projectionist, Pat, a Holywood man, was a fascinating and wonderful person to know; his philosophy on life always inspired those he came into contact with, making them think that little bit deeper about their thoughts and path in life. Apart from working at the cinema, some of Pat's hobbies were art, archery, singing and fencing. He was very talented artistically and was responsible for painting the various posters which were displayed inside and outside the cinema, informing the public of the various shows; this would include not only painting the lettering but also painting the images depicting the film. When watching Pat paint the cinema posters or pictures one was amazed at the ease and grace with which he used a paintbrush. Another gift Pat had was singing, belting out many of the old or then modern tunes, a favorite singer of his being the late Al Jolson. Many times I witnessed him captivating an audience in a musical melody of songs. On quite a few occasions after the show was over and everyone had gone home, Pat would turn on the stage spotlights and give me a rendition of songs like 'Old Man

River' on the cinema stage, and being the only member of the audience I got my pick of seats to watch from.

As a projectionist Pat knew the workings of his projectors back to front, and on many occasions when a film snapped or something went wrong with the sound or projector he quickly went into action and sorted out the problem. One of the first jobs when he arrived for a show would be to check he had the right film reel ready, which he threaded up on the projector; this was like an automatic process with him as he had done it so often over the years. He would then check the carbon rods were set up for the projector light. As the audience arrived, the curtain spotlights were turned on and the tape recorder was switched on for the background music, which was played until the show started.

Although Pat's job took place in the evenings, you could always catch sight of him during the day, darting in and out of the cinema getting something ready or working on a poster. One time I remember in particular, it was coming up to Christmas time and he used his artistic talents to produce a full-size Santa Claus out of wood, padding, clothing, cotton wool, etc. This was placed beside the traditional Christmas tree and was so realistic when it stood in the foyer that children would stand in amazement, waiting for it to come to life. Another excellent figure he produced was on the occasion of the film *Darby 0 'Gill and the Little People* being shown at the cinema in October 1968. He made a perfect little leprechaun about three feet high, dressed exactly as you would expect to see one. This was placed in the foyer standing behind a crock of imitation gold coins; this was like magic to children, drawing them in like a magnet. Dracula also made an appearance on one occasion, a full-size model made by Pat's hand. Patrons watched carefully as they passed it, waiting for it to grab them.

Pat was very well known throughout Holywood, and through the week there would be raps on the projection box door as various friends popped in to see him. One young man, Clifford, was a great film fanatic and he would call on a regular basis looking for old film display posters or little scraps of film that had broken off. Another friend was Harry; he was learning German and would regularly test his skills of the language on us, even though we hadn't a clue what he was talking about. Harry was a great accordion player and would entertain us every so often with a melody of tunes, and when a concert was held in the cinema he would always be there on stage as part of the entertainment.

The cinema was a part of Pat's life that he loved: making sure the films were ready, that the show started on time, his love of painting the posters for the forthcoming shows and the challenges that came with the job. With Pat, the show went on, and in all my years of involvement with the cinema I can never remember him failing to be there to start a film. Being the projectionist was a bit like being an entertainer: you were presenting the entertainment for the audience.

THE USHERS AND USHERETTES

The job of the usher/usherette dealt mainly with customer service, assisting people to their seats with the use of a flashlight, patrolling the aisles, checking tickets, managing queues, and so on.

Holywood Cinema usually had a male usher and a female usherette on duty; both were Holywood people. One remained at the main entrance and the other attended to the balcony, and for a period of time the main door usher had his own uniform.

If we were to provide a job description of the time it would probably cover the following:

- [ ] Being courteous and helpful to patrons.
- [ ] Greeting patrons.
- [ ] Checking tickets.
- [ ] Managing queues.
- [ ] Respond to complaints.
- [ ] Refusing admission to undesirables.
- [ ] Putting out undesirables.
- [ ] Asking people to be quiet during the show.
- [ ] Showing patrons the location of toilets and exit doors.
- [ ] Guiding patrons to their seats with the use of a flashlight.
- [ ] Making sure the fire exit doors were kept clear.
- [ ] Dealing with emergencies.

Obviously the job mainly involved evening work, except for the Saturday matinee. The usher/usherette was someone the younger people all feared to a certain degree, if doing something wrong. The usher on duty at the main entrance collecting tickets also looked after the ground floor auditorium. If not dealing with kids running about, talking, making nuisances of themselves or putting their feet up on the seats, he/she had to encounter the odd drunk rounding off their evening with a sleep before heading home, rarely seeing the film. Being local, the ushers knew most of the people coming into the cinema. Sometimes chips were secretly brought into the cinema and eaten whilst watching a film; this led to a strong aroma wafting through the cinema. The cinema shop done more business in the middle of a show, selling crisps and sweets.

Throughout almost every show, the light of the torch could be seen like a lighthouse beam in the middle of the night, piercing the darkness looking for a culprit that had perhaps thrown something at the screen or into the audience. Other than that, the torch was used to show people to their seats or find lost items. On occasions, the usher was summoned by a member of the audience to use their flashlight to retrieve a pair of glasses or purse that had fallen between the seats. I don't know if it was true, but I was told of a woman who was supposed to have lost the bottom half of her false teeth between the seats! During the busy times when the cinema was quite popular and there were queues, the usher would try and squeeze in as many people as possible; this meant squeezing in at the rear of the cinema, which made his job more difficult as he then had to get past everyone. The ushers had to be quite alert when there was a crowd as this was the time when people would try and slip in without a ticket. When you arrived late and the show had started, the one person you were glad to see was the usher who by the light of his/her torch would find a seat and direct you safely to it.

People enjoyed coming to the cinema, so unless someone became aggressive or was under the influence of alcohol the usher usually had a fairly peaceful shift. In most modern cinemas, to reduce costs, there are now no ushers except those taking your tickets on the way in. As an usher you had to be polite, positive and approachable as you dealt with a variety of people of all ages. One of the perks of the job was seeing all the latest movies being shown, the downside was that you had to stand for most of the night.

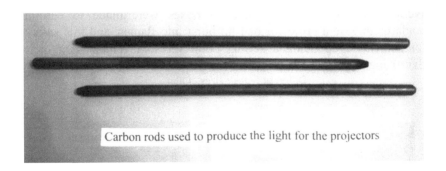

Carbon rods used to produce the light for the projectors

THE PROJECTION ROOM/BOX/BOOTH

The projection box was the hub of the cinema, like the engine room of a ship, and this was where all the entertainment came from. After ascending some very steep stairs and entering the dimly lit projection box, you were greeted by two giant projectors waiting, ready to entertain. The projectors were the original ones that had been installed when the cinema opened. The projection area itself was a bit like a concrete box, the purpose for this being to make it fireproof and to prevent sound from the projectors reaching the main auditorium. Years ago the film used in most cinemas was highly flammable; the film was cellulose nitrate, which eventually changed to cellulose acetate film. A number of people were killed in fires when film burst into flames upon exposure to a heat source. When burning, the film produced volumes of poisonous explosive gases – one memorable case happened in 1930 at the Glen Cinema in Paisley, Scotland. During a children's matinee the film caught fire in the projection box; the operator tried to carry the burning film outside but by this time smoke had engulfed the auditorium. As a result of this fire and smoke inhalation, 71 children died and 40 were injured. A safer type of film was eventually invented, but nonetheless projection boxes were made to certain standards in case a projector or film burst into flames, and this safety element ended up being a selling point for some cinemas in their advertising.

Different types / sizes of film

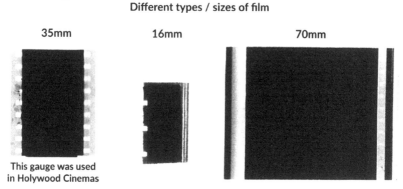

| 35mm | 16mm | 70mm |

This gauge was used
in Holywood Cinemas

21

The film gauge used in Holywood Cinema to show motion pictures was 35mm, and this was the standard gauge for most cinemas. Over the years it was changed and modified to retain colour, include sound, improve safety and take on a number of widescreen formats. The soundtrack ran down one side of the film and was picked up as it ran through the projector, being heard in sequence alongside the particular frames of film being shown. In today's cinemas this has all changed – with modernization came digital projectors.

The walls of the Holywood projection box were painted a dark blue, with an odd splash of coloured paint where Pat had perhaps wiped out a brush when painting a poster or something else. The furniture consisted of a small table which was usually covered in paper and brushes for the posters, a filing cabinet and one chair. Two long wooden platforms sat at the bottom of each projector to stand on so that you could reach the top spool carrier. On the wall in front of each projector were four holes filled with glass to suppress sound from the projectors, and it was through these that the films were projected onto the cinema screen and the operator was able to observe everything was correct. Pull-down shutters were built in; these would drop down if there was a fire. On the walls hung some fire extinguishers and in one corner there sat a fire bucket, full of sand.

A small door led into a storeroom, holding various bits and pieces such as Christmas decorations, carbon rods for the projectors and paper for making the weekly posters. Beside this another door opened to reveal steps which led down to the balcony stairs – these were used as an emergency fire escape exit, as were the main stairs. On a flat area halfway down the stairs some buckets, mops, brushes and cleaning materials were stored; these were the tools used by the cleaners for cleaning the cinema and toilets after the shows. Another doorway led into the spool room, where the films were stored.

The projectors themselves towered like two giant metal monsters, with cogs, wheels and spools all interlinked to help project the film onto the screen. A round compartment at the top of each machine had a door on it, into which the full film reel was placed; the film was then threaded down through various cogs and wheels, past the giant lens and onto an empty take-up spool at the bottom of the projector. As the film ran through, the pick-up reel retrieved the film onto the spool.

The terrific amount of light required to project the films was made through the joining of two carbon rods, a negative and a positive; the light was then reflected off a mirror and directed through the film. A lot of people used to believe the light came from a very large electric light bulb! An electric current passed through the rods and produced the intense light when they came together.

Checking the carbon rods

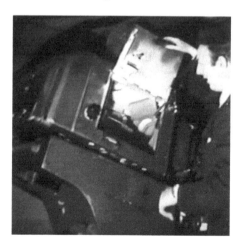

Throughout the showing of a film these rods would burn down, and not being able to move automatically, they had to be manually brought together by the turning of a knob to keep a constant light. If not done on time, this of course resulted in a variation of light, and anyone watching a film would notice a dulling of the picture. Unfortunately, this happened on odd occasions when the projectionist was getting the film reels ready. You could smell the rods burning away as they generated their powerful light, and they had to be changed on a regular basis depending on how quickly they burnt down, but it usually took about 45 minutes. In no time at all the bin would be filling up with the remains of burnt rods. Fumes from the burning rods were vented out through a steel chimney and onto the roof. Care had to be taken when handling the new boxes of rods – if dropped quite a few could be broken as they were so fragile. The light itself was reflected and focussed to where the film passed through and the projector lens was situated. When light shone through the lens the film was magnified and projected onto the cinema screen. Making a mistake could ruin a show for patrons, and so the projectionist had to ensure the right brightness on the screen, and that the picture was in focus and the sound adequate. There was no surround sound then – the sound came from behind the screen.

The 35mm film, when projected, used a very large lens to show it on the screen. Film composed of single pictures projected onto the screen at 24 frames per second, pausing briefly at each frame. Playing the film in rapid succession creates the illusion of movement. An entire film could consist of six or seven different reels which had to be run in succession without any breaks; this gave the appearance of the film being one continuous reel. The mystique of how the operation was done without showing any breaks in the film was interesting; if not done properly it could lead to the appearance of the film having bits cut out.

Films were normally collected from the distributors by 'the boss' and would arrive at the cinema in the boot of his car, consisting of a number of circular cans or metal boxes which then had to be carried up to the projection box. When carrying the film into the cinema you couldn't help reading the titles on the front of the canisters; you could be looking at a film about war, horror, adventure,love or a roll of Pathé News film, bringing news from around the world.

On an odd occasion when something went wrong and a breakage in the film occurred or film jammed in the projector, the cinema would erupt with clapping and shouts as the screen went blank. Pat then had to work frantically to rethread the film; at the same time, yards of film would be piling up on the floor until he was able to rewind it onto the take-up spool. A one-and-a-half-hour film could consist of about 5–6 reels with around 2,000 feet on each reel, and approximately every 15–20 minutes, when a reel was coming to the end, the projectionist had to already have threaded up the next reel on the second projector, ready to change over to it. Watching carefully at the top corner of the screen, a small star or dot could be seen for a few seconds near the end of a reel; this was the sign for the projectionist to start up the second projector with the new reel. Upon seeing a second dot appear on the screen the projectionist pulled a lever, putting the second projector into operation and at the same time cutting off the first.

There could, of course, be a problem when doing this if the projectionist missed the cue to change over. This would result in the first reel running out and a blank screen appearing; the audience would soon let you know when this had happened. A changeover at the wrong time could also give the impression that something had been missed from the film, and the claims made when going home after the show would be that the cinema staff cut part of the film out and the patrons did not get their money's worth, even though the missing frames amounted to only a few seconds.

When a reel had gone through the projector, it was only a matter of rewinding the reel ready to show it again at the next screening. One nightmare you hoped would never happen was that, with having only two projectors, one would break down; another was if you put on the wrong reel out of sequence.

So the sequence for starting a show was:

1   At the start of a show, before a film was shown, the carbon rods had to be in place and the film threaded through the projector.
2   The film reel was checked to make sure it was the right reel.
3   The houselights were turned off, and the spotlights that shone on the screen curtain were dimmed before being turned off by pulling a large switch down.
4   A flick of another switch raised the curtain as the film started running through the machine.
5   Another handle on the projector was pulled forward, releasing the light from the carbon rods through the film, and bingo! The show had started.

Once a film had been shown it was then only a matter of rewinding the film to a start position ready for the next show or winding it off its reel to be sent back to the distributor.

THE SPOOL ROOM

At the other end of the projection box, walking through brought you to the spool room where the films were stored and wound to and from the projector spools.

In this room, a small window gave a wonderful view right down the High Street as far as the Maypole. A sturdy wooden table held a hand-operated spool-winding machine. From the spool room access could be made to the roof of the cinema, to a wonderful view over Holywood and Belfast Lough. Dotted about were small frames of film where a film had broken and had to be cut in order to cement the parts together again. There were also small rolls of film that contained trailers and advertisements that had to be attached or had been shown with the latest film.

The spool room had to be kept clean and dust free, dust could damage and scrape the emulsion which would then show up as scrapes when magnified on to the screen. The drinking of tea or liquids was not generally allowed in case it was accidently spilt on to the film.

There were no actual shelves in the spool room, films were simply stacked up vertically on their reel or left in the metal case they came in until being used. The metal cases usually took up more room than quite a few reels. One had to be careful when new films arrived and the used ones had not been removed in case you lifted out the wrong reel to project.

When films arrived at the cinema, the spool room was where they ended up. They arrived in their metal cans and had to be prepared before showing, the loose film being wound onto metal reels ready for projection. Films had to be checked in case they were damaged when you received them: this could be splices that had become unstuck; damage to the sprocket holes that helped feed the film through the projector; or missing sections of film. Some cinemas had a special book in which the condition of film upon delivery was recorded so that they would not get blamed for any damage. Scratches on film would show up on the screen so care had to be taken when handling it.

Winding the films was done manually on the two-geared wheels, using a large handle to turn them. A spool of film was placed on one wheel and an empty spool on the other, and after threading the film onto the empty spool it was only a matter of turning the handle. Quite a speed could be achieved when turning the handle, but this would soon slow down after turning a few reels as you quickly ran out of energy. One of the worst things that could happen after winding a film off the spool ready to be returned to the distributor was when the film, which seemed endless, suddenly had the centre fall out, followed by yards and yards of film falling straight onto the floor. This meant having to manually rewind the whole roll; this was your worst nightmare and seemed like a never-ending job – I speak from experience.

For occasions when a film broke or tore, there was a small 'splicer' kit available which stuck the two parts together again. Film cement was used to weld the two broken pieces. A clear, smooth cut was made at the end of each broken piece of film and the emulsion scraped off; the cement was applied and then the two pieces of film pressed together in the splicer to form a weld, which you hoped would stay stuck. Sometimes film would break in the middle of a reel during playback; this was mostly due to a joint that had been made when the film broke some time before suddenly coming apart. Joints were also made when trailers or advertisements were added on. When the screen went blank due to a film breakage, or any other reason, a report had to be made to the cinema manager.

As well as the aforementioned, some of the reasons why a joint would come apart were:

☐   Too much of a delay in putting the two pieces together after cement had been applied.
☐   Too little cement being applied.
☐   Not being left to dry for long enough, resulting in the ends parting.

You had to be careful with the spools that held the film. These were quite heavy and if dropped could be damaged; this could result in the film not winding on or off the spool smoothly, which could lead to possible damage to the film or problems when projecting it. When there were a lot of reels it was important to make sure that they were not mixed up as this would completely change the plot of a film. This meant holding the film up to the light and checking to make sure you had the right reel.

THE CINEMA SCREEN

In those days in Holywood we had nothing like the surround sound that is now available in cinemas, which gives the appearance of the audience being enveloped in the sound. The cinema screen, although it looked solid, was full of tiny holes which let the sound through from speakers that were mounted at the rear of the screen, making the sound seem to come from the person speaking at the time. Different screens are known by the amount of light they reflected to the viewer. There were pearl, silver, matte white and glass beaded screens, which were made of a type of heavy white vinyl stretched across a frame.

When there was a Cinemascope film to be shown, the size of the screen had to be adjusted. This meant a black masking cloth being moved to block out and change part of the screen to suit the size of the film. In modern cinemas this would probably be done with the flick of a switch; but unfortunately we did not have that luxury, and this meant walking through the cinema to the rear of the screen and manually pulling the masking cloth up or down by the use of a rope.

When the picture was over, the reverse had to be done to return the screen to its normal size. The rear of the projection screen was a very dark place, so when working there this was a job you did not look forward to and hence was done with great speed, particularly if the film showing was a horror picture. Now and again parts of the screen had to be cleaned with a damp cloth after someone from the audience had thrown something against it. It has been known for some cinemas in the past just to have a painted wall to project the film onto instead of a screen.

HOLYWOOD CINEMA   PHONE 3283   Friday and Saturday THE GREAT RACE

MONDAY 1st MAY   FOR SIX DAYS

Paramount film returns triumphant, complete and uncut

CHARLTON HESTON—THE TEN COMMANDMENTS

Owing to length of film (3 hours 40 minutes) one showing nightly

Doors open 6.30, commencing 7.00

THE FOYER

Walking through the main entrance doors brought you into the entrance foyer where the cashier's ticket box was situated. This consisted of a small framed box and glass front with enough room for one person, a seat and a ticket machine. Money was handed to Molly, the smiling cashier, through a small hole at the front of the glass partition, and then she pushed a lever which resulted in a ticket popping up, which you gleefully grabbed as your passport to a few hours of pleasure. The mechanism for the machine was fairly old but still effective, churning out ticket after ticket. When there were queues, the cashier was kept quite busy, often ending up in a scrambling match when the large roll of tickets came to an end and had to be replenished.

One extra job for the cashier and ushers was to be observant and watch out for undesirables who had been put out on previous occasions and banned, perhaps for being rowdy or getting up to some other form of mischief, as well as people who were underage for the particular film that was showing. As well as this, when some children who had paid for tickets for the main auditorium saw the cashier was busy, they would try and slip up the stairs to the balcony, only to be nabbed by whoever was up there taking tickets, or by Mr Turner, the manager, who would quickly dispatch them downstairs again. On a few occasions when working in the cinema, I came across one or two lads gingerly creeping up the stairs towards the balcony, quickly doing a U-turn when they heard my footsteps.

The walls in the foyer were painted a light grey colour and the doors a dark blue; this colour scheme extended up two separate sets of stairs to the balcony. A door in the corner of the foyer led to the toilets, and at the other side (as mentioned earlier) there was a glass partition through which you could purchase sweets from the cinema shop.

Although both staircases leading from the foyer ended up at the balcony, one of the staircases also brought you up to the door of the projection box, and the other passed a door leading to the manager's office. Because of the concrete walls there was a sort of echo when you spoke on the stairs. There were times, when there w a s a popular film on, that people ended up queuing in the foyer as well as out through the doors and onto the footpath.

On the ground floor two large doors led from the foyer into the cinema auditorium, and on the same wall there was a glass frame for posters showing the latest films. After reaching this area in the cinema, an air of excitement was palpable – only two doors stood between you and certain adventure!

THE AUDITORIUM

Auditoriums were built to allow audiences to see and hear performances, be it in a theatre or in a cinema. The floor in the cinema was sloped, meaning each seat was slightly higher than the one in front to allow you to see over the person in front's head.

Before going into the main auditorium, patrons' tickets were handed to a member of staff and torn; the large doors were then pulled open for admission to the show. A wood-and-glass screen with red curtains was the first thing that met you when you entered the auditorium – this was basically to cut down any breeze coming in, and the curtains were to stop light getting in from outside when the doors were opened. When there was a queue you would have to stand at this screen, peering through the glass and jostling to see the film until a seat became vacant. Turning left or right brought you into the main body of the cinema. Two aisles and a gently sloping floor brought you down through the auditorium, where lines of red seats lay on each side of you as you made your way to your seat. If the lights were out an usherette directed you by the light of a torch.

The tip-up seats themselves were covered in red upholstery material and were very basic compared to today's cinema seating. After an hour or so they were not the most comfortable, and you had to keep changing position to avoid becoming numb. Because the distance between the rows of seats was so narrow, every time someone wanted to go to the toilet or shop most people in the row had to stand up, to the annoyance of people sitting beside or behind. Modern-day cinema seats have a special hole in the armrest for placing your drink, but in those days (if you could afford it) you had to juggle a bottle of lemonade and a bag of sweets on your knee at the same time, and as soon as the person next to you removed their arm from the wooden armrest you planted your elbow on it promptly to get your turn on it.

Between each seat there was a little metal ashtray for smokers – smoking was allowed then, much to the annoyance of anyone sitting beside you who didn't smoke; during the show you would see the smoke curling up into the ceiling through the light of the projector. Seats in the balcony area were slightly better in that the elbow rest was covered in material, but space between the seats was kept to a minimum, no doubt to fit in more seats, making it awkward when you wanted to make an exit or entry. There was nothing overly ornate about the ceiling and walls of the auditorium – they were mostly plain in design.

Overhead, when at the rear of the cinema, you were covered by the overhanging balcony, something which not all cinemas had. At the rear of the balcony was a toilet, and a trapdoor in the ceiling led you into the roof space. When looking into it, the roof space was like a large black void containing dust, ducting and the remains of old original lead gas pipes, although modern electrical wiring and piping were also present.

As you walked further down past the rows of seats in the auditorium, the cinema opened up, giving an all-round view of the entire interior. On the odd occasion this could be a dangerous area when seated and watching a film, as you were liable to be hit on the head with a stubbed-out cigarette butt, lollipop stick or crumpled-up sweet paper that had been fired from somewhere in the crowd or the balcony above. The cinema had its own aroma; I still don't know if this was from the seats or the cleaning materials used.

Before working at the cinema, when my friends and I had gathered up enough money to pay for a balcony seat we would gleefully head to the cinema with great anticipation. To us this was where the rich people sat – no rowdies (well, not always), more luxurious seats (or should I say arm rests) and no straining your neck to watch the film.

Over the years individuals from all walks of life came to the cinema: shop assistants, shipyard workers, business people, housewives, children, husbands and wives, lovers, families and groups, all looking to spend a few hours escaping the humdrum of normal life.

Originally the screen was covered by the traditional red curtains which parted to each side; later, when modernized, these were replaced with yards and yards of gold-coloured curtains which rose upwards and made the cinema look very modern. There was always a great feeling of anticipation when sitting looking at the curtains, as you knew that as soon as the spotlight faded they would rise up and you would enter the world of entertainment. Two new spotlights were put up at the same time the curtains were changed, and when these shone on the curtains a golden brilliance radiated from them. Some modern cinemas don't even have curtains or ushers anymore –You make your own way to your seat which has a number on it.

When waiting for the show to start, background music was played; this normally consisted of the same recording that was played from the projection box and was recorded on an old reel-to-reel tape recorder – one favorite catchy tune I can always remember being played regularly was 'The Bottle Theme'. This was the time to look around and see who you knew, and make a mad dash between the seats to talk to someone you hadn't seen for a while.

HOLYWOOD CINEMA

Before a picture began, sometimes all that could be heard was the sound of voices chattering and the rustle of sweet papers. When the lights dimmed and the curtain went up some people had to be reminded to be quiet, as they were so engrossed in catching up with the latest news or gossip. Sometimes the heating in the cinema was not turned on if it was thought the temperature was fine, or it might not have warmed up properly by the time a film started, which might on a cold night mean everyone wrapped their coats a bit tighter around themselves – a good excuse for young lovers to snuggle a bit closer. Ice lollies did not sell too well on a night like this! By the time the film was nearing an end, the cinema was starting to warm up. The heating system was quite old, having been in the cinema since it opened, and it was eventually replaced in 1968 with a more modern system. I can remember two women (who were regulars) who would bring a small rug with them, just in case.

Many romantic first dates took place at the cinema, and it also served as a meeting place for friends to enjoy an evening together. By viewing the audience on a regular basis before the show started, you could see the same people following the same habits in that they always headed for the same seats or area when they arrived for a show. Courting couples would all make a beeline for the double seats situated halfway down the aisle, others headed to the rear seats, as did those who liked to make a quick exit at the end of the show after the national anthem was played. Some of those who would be termed 'rowdies' would head for the front row seats, although most people avoided these as it meant ending up with a sore neck from looking up all through the show. Ending up in the front seats could also mean sitting on a slashed seat where someone had decided to take a knife to it. Unfortunately, if the cinema was full this was where you could end up. The average person made for the centre row where they could look straight at the screen; patrons on the right or left aisles had to look left or right to a degree as they were slightly facing from the side of the screen.

There was always the odd person who, when watching a film with their friend or relative, would continuously describe what was happening on the screen – much to the annoyance of the other person

– despite the fact the other person was watching exactly the same film at exactly the same time!

In those days we certainly got value for money in that we saw two films and probably also a cartoon per show, rather than the traditional one film we get nowadays. This meant that there was a short or supporting film, which we called the 'wee picture' or 'B movie'. These were films that were made on a smaller budget, and a lot of them were in black and white. A lot of wonderful pictures were made at Ealing Studios in England, although more and more American films started appearing in colour until eventually you only saw the odd black-and-white one. After the 'wee picture' there was then usually a break with Pathé News giving all the latest news from around the world. As not everyone had the luxury of television, this was most people's way of catching up with what was happening; otherwise they had to listen to it on the radio. The Pathé newsreel started off with a crowing cockerel on the screen. Some of the newsreel companies operating throughout Britain at the time were British Movietone, Universal, Paramount and Pathé News. In the then not too distant future, newsreels were to disappear along with supporting films. After the newsreel, there was a variety of advertisements from Pearl & Dean for things like cars, cigars and cigarettes, followed by the coming attractions – previews for films that were going to be shown in the next few weeks. This was followed by the 'big picture' or main feature film. When the advertisements were screened this would be the time to get stocked up on sweets, if you hadn't already; for a time a young lady would appear down near the screen carrying a special tray with a battery light that lit up the various delights within the tray, such as Lyons Maid ice cream, lollies, sweets and drinks. The ice cream came in a little tub with a small wooden spoon. You had to be quick as there was an instant rush of people and everything disappeared rapidly; however, there was also the cinema sweet shop if the queue got too long. It was quite amusing to see people nip out to the shop in the break when the lights were on only to come back in when the lights were out and the show had restarted; they could then be seen wandering up and down the aisle in the dark, trying to find their seats and hoping a friend would wave at them as they stumbled along.

A few of the films that were advertised appeared to be a bit of a disappointment after watching the entire film. Some people believed all the best bits were sometimes shown on the trailer and perhaps these may have been the only exciting parts of the film! However, there was always a good variety of films to suit all tastes: war films, westerns, science fiction films, gangster films, romances, murder mysteries, cartoons and comedies. Films that starred Laurel and Hardy, Charlie Chaplin or the Bowery Boys had the audience in fits of laughter; a good romance had tears rolling and a film starring Elvis Presley had the girls swooning.

If you were a young boy or girl one thing that could sometimes annoy you was when adults were sitting in front of you, blocking your view of the screen. When this happened there was no alternative but to tip up your seat and sit on top of the edge, as although eventually sore on the legs, this gave you a great view of the screen and all around the cinema. You had to be alert, however, as this was frowned upon because you were then blocking the view of someone behind you, as well as perhaps damaging the seat, and so constant watch was kept for cinema staff.

As mentioned before, you could smoke in buildings at the time, and throughout the cinema in the darkness could be seen little spots of light, like fairy lights, as people drew on their cigarettes. Unfortunately, this meant holes in the lino and carpet due to people carelessly stubbing out their cigarette butts. Because the cinema was so large, unless you were actually sitting next to someone smoking the smoke was not as noticeable as you would expect in a small, confined space; however, we now know that second-hand smoke may have been inhaled unwillingly by anyone sitting beside a smoker.

Something the usher had to watch out for was the favourite trick of children who did not have the money to get into the cinema. They would club together so that one would have enough money to get in, then just as the show started you would see one of them who was sitting down near the front disappear in the direction of the toilets, only to reappear a minute later with two or three others. As they headed to the toilets, they would open the rear exit doors leading to Downshire Road and let their friends in, closing the doors again and returning to their seat as though returning from the toilets. On odd occasions some of the younger members of the audience would sometimes be put out in the middle of a film for continuous talking, carrying on or perhaps firing rolled-up paper at other people in the audience or at the screen. If you were seated near them when this was going on you ducked down as far as you could in your seat, trying not to be noticed in case you were blamed. Although the ushers may have appeared very intimidating to wrongdoers, they were really very pleasant people and just doing their job.

Another thing young people used to hate was when an X-rated film was being shown, as this meant you were banned from getting in, being underage. These films were mostly horror and sex-related films that had been X-rated so that you had to be a certain age to view them. At some horror films you used to see the odd young person who would arrive at the cinema with an adult or wait outside for an adult they knew to come along and, pretending they were under their care, try and gain admission, only to still be refused entry when they reached the ticket kiosk. When you look back now, compared to the films that have appeared in more recent years, some of those films were actually quite mild in content.

Somewhere people would head before coming into the cinema, rather than going to the cinema shop, was Elliotts – a sweet shop just around the corner from the cinema. Elliotts was run by two sisters, and situated at the bottom of Downshire Road beside what was then Moffett's, the butchers. Elliotts' old shop was eventually turned into what was known as the Holywood Dental Laboratory; in years to come it was demolished when the dental lab moved to opposite St

Helens. There was also a video rental shop there at one time. One of the favorites to be found in Elliotts was a chocolate fudge bar called a Whopper bar; this had lots of chewing built into it, and because they were cheap a few of them kept you chewing at least to the end of the 'wee picture'. Another favorite was the gobstopper, this lasted for ages when sucked and seemed everlasting. Although in a lot of modern cinemas popcorn is a very popular treat, it was not such a big thing in the 1960s at Holywood Cinema.

When a show had ceased and the flickering light of the projector stopped, the curtains had closed and the audience had left, the cleaners converged on the empty seats and aisles tipping up the seats to expose a variety of rubbish. This could consist of cigarette butts, empty crisp bags, sweet papers, chewing gum, lollipop sticks, coins, paper money and the occasional purse, glasses or handbag that had been forgotten. After weaving their way through the seats it wasn't long before the empty crisp boxes used to collect the rubbish were full to the brim.

Once the cleaners were finished, the cinema returned to a place of total silence – time became still again until the next evening when film stars and the public mingled once again.

After the show friends and families could be seen scurrying along home in the dark, in conversation about the film they had just seen, and some of them still mentally lingering on playing the part of the hero.

MATINEES

When young everyone looked forward in anticipation to the Saturday matinee in the cinema, arriving with perhaps your pocket money for the week, balancing it out between tickets for the show and sweets. The matinee used to take place around 11.00am, but at one time it was at 2.00pm. This was a time when children could squeal and shout without having being told off by their parents. As everyone entered the cinema there was a mad dash for seats as friends tried to sit together in the same row. The noise could be deafening before the start of the show as they talked, shouted and played over the seats and up and down the aisle. Once the start of a film hit the screen there would be a deafening roar from them all.

For the matinees there was usually a main picture such as a western, a cartoon and a serial shown. Films such as Roy Rogers, Tom & Jerry or Disney films were quite popular; these were supported by a serial film such as Flash Gordon starring Larry 'Buster' Crabbe as Flash. Every week faithful followers watched such episodes as 'Space Soldiers Conquer The Universe', with every episode ending in a nail-biting cliff hanger that had you talking with your friends about it all week until the following Saturday, when it started all over again. Large cheers erupted when a villain was killed or captured, as well as jumping up and down on the seats (much to the annoyance of the cinema staff). Films starring Abbott and Costello, the Bowery Boys or Charlie Chaplin, and the cartoons, kept you in fits of laughter.

Not all the cinema lights were turned out so it was possible to see who you were throwing a lollipop stick at, if that way inclined, but it also made the ushers' job easier in that they could see you. Staff certainly had their hands full with children jumping on and over the seats, running in and out to the shop and constantly talking or shouting. There was also the odd fight that broke out. This was why they were all herded into one part of the cinema and some of the lights were left on so that they could be surrounded by staff and watched. The same children normally attended the matinee each week, not wanting to miss the nail-biting episode of whatever serial was showing. Some major cinemas had a minors club for children; they had their own songs, badges and compère.

When the show had finished a mini screeching crowd dashed for the exit, everyone trying to get out first. Cleaners then had their work cut out gathering sweet papers, lollipop sticks and sticky chewing gum from between the seats.

After the matinee on a Saturday, depending on the film shown, youngsters could be seen dodging behind hedges or walls when going home, playing at shooting each other after watching a cowboy film, or with the aid of two sticks fencing each other just as they had seen in a film about knights. The acting when someone was killed was pure Oscar material! If they had enough money, some k i d s would head down to Tog's on the High Street and purchase some of Tog's delicious homemade ice cream or lemonade.

SHOWS AND TALENT COMPETITIONS

During the cinema's existence, and later as audiences started to decline, cinemas tried different ideas to bring customers back to the cinema, such as shows, late films, bingo, etc. Holywood Cinema was no exception, and the small stage at the front was extended outwards to accommodate groups, singers and artists. Late-night film shows were put on regularly, and on nearly every weekend in 1969 there was a late-night show, usually on a Friday night. A lot of these would be horror or X-rated films to bring in the audiences, and because it was unusual to have entertainment that late at night they became quite popular.

May 1964 saw a late-night show entitled *Big Beat '64* (with various artists). This turned out to be quite a success, with appearances from artists such as The Recordites, Brian Rossi and three rhythm groups: Lee Parker and the Vibratones, The Kentuckians and Vaqueros. There were also talent competitions, with local singers and musicians providing entertainment and hoping for stardom – this live entertainment drew in people from all around Holywood and afar and was very well attended. One particular two-man group from Holywood stands out in my mind: Harry Irwin and Fred Bell – Harry used to play the accordion along with Fred on the drums. Harry could be seen at quite a few birthdays, shows, etc. around Holywood, entertaining with a melody of tunes.

Also in 1964, the cinema ran a major talent competition that was attended by a variety of artists over the weeks. On the final night in March, the first prize of £20 went to a Conlig group called The Delvaros; the second prize of £10 was won by Angela Patton from Belfast; and the third prize of £5 went to Holywood girl Jennifer McConnell who sang 'Just for You' and 'The Wedding'. Compère for the show was Tom Martin, the drummer from the television show *Tea Time with Tommy*. As well as the potential stars from the talent competition, other artists appeared including Frank Carson, the popular Recordites with George Carroll and Sid Dodsworth, and local projectionist Pat Malone, who entertained the audience with his versions of Al Jolson hits. The raffle was run in aid of the USPCA, with prizes being supplied by Mr G. Brady, Mr E. Allen, Mr T. Lundy and Holywood Cinema management. The cash prizes provided by Holywood Cinema were considered to be very substantial at the time.

A very popular entertainer throughout the cinemas and clubs in Northern Ireland, including Holywood Cinema, was the wonderful Edwin Heath, the hypnotist. On occasions, when not playing in Belfast or elsewhere, he appeared with his own show and mesmerised numerous people after solidly locking their hands together. The stage then ended up covered with bodies doing all sorts of weird, strange and funny antics. 1968 was a popular year in the cinemas for Edwin – March brought him to Holywood Cinema for a midnight matinee. In July of that year he then appeared at the Queens Cinema in Bangor; this show was entitled *The Great Edwin Heath Show* and lasted for a full week. In November of the same year he brought a two-night show back to Holywood Cinema, supported by a variety of artists. Admission to the show was 4s and the balcony seats could be booked for 5s.

Edwin went on to travel across the high seas every year on the massive cruise liners, entertaining guests before returning home to carry out the odd show or privately provide hypnotherapy sessions for those who required them. The shows were filled each night and amounted to very enjoyable entertainment. Edwin was what would be called a gentleman: captivating, courteous and fascinating to speak to. It was amusing to see how many people were afraid to be introduced to him and would deliberately avoid him, thinking he would instantly put them to sleep or under his spell.

Conlig group The Delvaros who won first prize
(Photo: Courtesy of the *County Down Spectator*)

Other late-night film shows and talent competitions took place over the years, all attracting a good audience, particularly from Holywood. But eventually audiences started dwindling, making it financially uneconomical to continue. The cinema then returned to just showing films.

REDECORATION

One year, it was decided that the interior of the cinema should be refurbished; this involved redecoration, installation of a new heating system and general repairs. The cinema was closed for one week from

Monday 12th February 1968 for the work to be carried out, and obviously for as long as the cinema was closed there was no revenue coming in, so the redecoration and repairs had to be carried out as quickly as possible.

Decorating the cinema was quite a big job and required a large scaffolding platform to be set up to reach the very high ceiling and walls. The well-known Holywood painting firm of Wm. Stevenson & Sons, who were established in Holywood in 1911, were called in to undertake the job. They had the experience of painting most of the larger buildings around Holywood over the years. A small squad of painters were involved, using gallons and gallons of paint and painting one large square at a time before having to move the scaffolding; a slow, laborious job, particularly as everything had to be undercoated and then painted over again.

Hugh and Sammy Stevenson organized the assault and, to get the job done in time, evening overtime was essential. Some rows of seats had to be removed to allow the scaffolding to be moved about, but even so it was very awkward to move and resulted in a lot of puffing and blowing. The complete interior of the cinema was painted, including the ceiling and walls along with the toilets and also both staircases. Whilst the repainting was being carried out a new heating system was also installed, which meant all sorts of other workmen walking through the cinema, carrying tools and lots of piping, banging on pipes and causing dust and noise, much to the annoyance of the painters. It was also an opportunity to fix and mend broken seats, with damaged ones being replaced or cleaned. Near the front of the cinema whole rows of seats had to be reattached to the floor; they had been loosened due to people putting their feet on the rear of the seats in front and pushing.

The smell of paint lingered throughout the auditorium for weeks after the job was finished, and radiators in particular (when heated up) produced a stronger smell, which was why, even if they were cold, people avoided sitting beside them for quite a while. Overall the cinema looked wonderful when the job was completed, and it reopened on Monday 19th February. The film showing at this time for a full six days was *The Dirty Dozen*.

CENSORSHIP

Censorship rules were brought into effect to protect people, and in particular young people, from being exposed to films which were regarded as being unsuitable. These could be films of a sexual nature, horror films or violence, human rights violations, use of drugs, etc. Censorship was usually carried out by The British Board of Censorship or local and borough councils.

In the 1960s censorship ratings were changed and the following came into effect:

- G – General audiences, suitable for all ages.
- PG – Parental guidance suggested.
- R – Restricted to no one under 16 unless accompanied by an adult.
- X – For 16 years and over.

Cinema staff had to be observant of these rules as the cinema could get into trouble for admitting persons who were underage. It was sometimes difficult to determine ages and few people brought a form of identification along with them. Staff had to rely basically on visual appearance and honesty.

BANNED

In December 1973 a new film called *The Exorcist* was released in America. Being a horror film it hit the headlines all over America because of its content, and at some cinemas there was an ambulance or nurse on standby in case people became ill after watching it. When the film eventually reached Northern Ireland the publicity followed it. Now, compared to its modern-day equals, *The Exorcist* would probably be classed by some as fairly mild for a horror film.

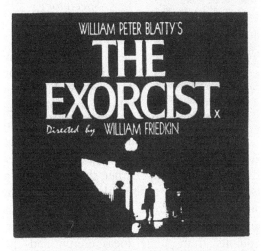

Keep this leaflet.

You may need it later.

WILLIAM PETER BLATTY'S

THE EXORCIST x

Directed by WILLIAM FRIEDKIN

"Some people who never before needed mental treatment were falling apart after seeing this film"

– The Western Psychiatric Institute, Pittsburg, U.S.A. after admitting 12 new patients.

The Exorcist was booked to be shown for six days at Holywood Cinema. The film had previously been shown in Bangor at the Queens Cinema for six days and at the Regent Cinema in Newtownards for two weeks. However, at a special meeting of North Down Borough Council, after much debate, it was decided by seven votes to five that the film should be banned from being shown in Holywood Cinema. The fact that the film had not been banned in Bangor or Newtownards was discussed, and it was also debated as to why the council should ban the film when the British Board of Film Censors had not banned it.

John Turner, the manager on the night *The Exorcist* was being shown
(Photo: Courtesy of the *County Down Spectator*)

On a Monday night in April 1975 the film was screened at Holywood Cinema. The North Down Council enforcement officer was in attendance on the Monday night to make sure that no one under censorship age had been allowed in. John Turner then received a telephone call on the Tuesday night from a councilor informing him that the show had been banned. This was to be followed up by a letter from the council. North Down District Council had decided to ban the film after receiving complaints from some local clergy and the Holywood & District Community Association.

According to reports from one religious group, the showing of the film had produced disturbing effects in people who had watched it, including a woman fainting in the street in Newtownards immediately after seeing the film and psychiatric care being needed for another young person in Bangor. Mr. Turner had no choice but to close the cinema as it was too late to book another film.

(Photo: Courtesy of the *County Down Spectator*)

That night, however, because of all the publicity about the film, a queue of around 100 people had formed outside the cinema to see the film, and they were getting quite impatient – some of them began banging on the doors. Police were advised in case there was going to be any trouble. There were quite a lot of soldiers in the queue from the nearby Palace Barracks, and with advice from a fellow director and the possibility of losing his license, Mr. Turner informed a member of the council that he was going ahead and showing the film, which he did. Mr. R. Turner, brother of John Turner and a director of Holywood Cinema, commented that it was very narrow-minded of the council to allow people in Bangor to see the film and not those in Holywood.

At a follow-up meeting of North Down Borough Council it was decided not to take any action against Mr. Turner for defying the ban, as given that the film had already been shown for two nights and the ban was on such short notice, it would not have been fair. It was remarked, however, that the council would look in particular at the cinema's license when it next came up for renewal. Some councilors believed that they had in some respect made fools of themselves. Interestingly, in 1975 when the renewal of the cinematograph license was up for approval the question was asked whether the council had any control over the standards of films shown in cinemas. The answer given was that the license applied solely to the storing of inflammable celluloid film.

48

Whether *The Exorcist* affected anyone mentally or whether they were physically sick I do not know; however, the ban resulted in more publicity for the film and for Holywood Cinema.

UNSEEN VISITORS?

The cinema itself, when empty of patrons and staff, was quite an eerie place to wander around on your own. On quite a few occasions when a show was over and silence fell about the building Pat and I, who were finishing off, would suddenly glance at each other, wondering if the other had just heard the same sound. We found our ears being strained quite a few times upon suddenly hearing a bang from somewhere or the sound of a door closing, and we would automatically think that this was due to the central heating cooling down, ignoring (or forgetting) the fact that it was not on! On a few occasions we were so convinced there was someone in the cinema other than ourselves that we turned on all the lights and made a complete search.

There was one occasion that could not be put down to central heating. The story was related to me by Pat himself. At the rear end of the cinema, behind the screen, was an upstairs loft in which Pat used to work on his posters. On one occasion, during the middle of the day, Pat was working in the loft when he suddenly heard the sound of footsteps coming down the aisle – nothing unusual, except that there was no one else in the cinema! All the lights were out in the auditorium, the front doors were firmly locked and there was no one in the building. He called out, and the footsteps stopped but no one answered. So he continued working, believing his imagination was a bit hazy, but as he continued he distinctly heard the footsteps again. After calling out again the footsteps stopped, and very gingerly he climbed down the ladder and slowly opened the door leading into the auditorium. Peering out into the inky darkness, he could see and hear nothing. At this stage he had a very strong feeling of extreme coldness from his head to his toes. Taking a deep breath, he dashed into the darkness, hitting the edge of each seat to help him feel his way towards the dimly lit exit doors. Upon reaching the foyer he immediately checked the front doors to find them securely locked.

Then, after turning on all the lights in the auditorium, he carefully checked the whole cinema and found nothing. With the cinema now gone, we shall of course never know the cause of this experience.

PRICES

It is interesting to note the prices of the admission charges for the cinema.
Below is a sample of prices and how they changed over the years:

Holywood Cinema prices:

1936 – 3d to 1s.3d
1955 – 1s to 2s.3d
1966 – 1s.6d to 2s.6d
1970 – 2s.6d to 3s.6d

Here we see a snapshot of some 1969 price comparisons, the larger cinemas appeared to charge a bit extra:

Holywood Cinema – 1s.6d to 2s.6d
Tonic, Bangor – 4s to 5s
Curzon, Belfast – 3s to 5s
Odeon, Belfast – 6s to 7s
Palace, L/Derry – 2s.6d to 5s
Frontier, Newry – 2s to 2s.6d
Regent, Newtownards – 1s.6d to 3s.6d

New Cinema

HOLYWOOD

Maypole Cinema
Holywood   Phone 285

THE CINEMA PROGRAMME

A printed programme was produced by the cinema on a regular basis, giving details of films to be shown over the coming month. As there were three different shows a week, having a programme was handy to see the choice of films available. The programme was available for free at the kiosk when obtaining your ticket. Revenue was generated from the production of the programme as local businesses advertised in it, for a fee. As soon as the programmes were produced, they were quickly snapped up by patrons who came in to see a show.

There was no internet at the time through which to advertise, so the cinema found other forms of advertising in local papers such as the *Spectator*, on posters around the cinema and at various other locations around Holywood. The *Spectator* presented a weekly view of what was available and also a column which gave a rundown on what the films were about. The cinema advertised in the *Spectator* up until around May 1971.

If you didn't have a programme, information about films that were available was usually passed on by word of mouth. Most people

52

probably looked at the posters on the front of the cinema when walking or driving past. An experience at one of the poster locations, beside a local garage, where Pat (the projectionist) used to change the poster on a weekly basis, left him with a habit of pulling down the old poster and quickly stepping back – experience had shown him that when he pulled down the old poster he got showered with a mass of insects!

Eventually the cinema stopped producing programmes and the only advertising was on the front of the cinema.

FILMS

The majority of films, similar to television programmes, were in black and white for a period before colour became more common. American films made quite a change – showing lavish scenery and colour, and apparently no expense was spared on any action or special effects scenes.

The variety of films shown in the cinema stretched from one extreme to the other. A lot of these films starred actors and actresses who were either just starting their careers or well established as film stars at the time. Sherlock Holmes and Miss Marple films were quite popular, as were Disney films. Various films enticed different cinemagoers, all having their own taste in films. One man in particular would only come to the cinema when there was a war film showing.

To attract adult audiences there were some foreign X-rated films which had subtitles at the bottom of the screen. Horror films included X-rated films such as *Dracula, Frankenstein, The Wolf Man* and *The Mummy*, usually made and distributed by Hammer and Universal Films. These, we thought, were absolutely frightening; they had people jumping in their seats or cowering behind them. It was amusing to see some girls covering their faces with their hands when something scary was happening, but all the time they were peering between their fingers at the film. If they were out with their boyfriends, this was an opportunity to get that bit closer. On a dark night, after seeing one of these films, many people walking home made sure they stayed well out of the shadows!

54

Monday 1st. Two days
William Holden . Nancy Kwan
THE WORLD OF SUZIE WONG

Wednesday 3rd. Two days
Robert Taylor . Julie London
SADDLE THE WIND
Richard Eyer—INVISIBLE BOY

Friday 5th. Two days
Pat Boone . Buddy Hackett
Dennis O'Keefe
ALL HANDS ON DECK
David Hedison
THE EMERALD CURTAIN

Monday 8th. Two days
Anthony Perkins . Vera Miles
John Gavin — P S Y C H O

Wednesday 10th. Two days
Danny Kaye . Dana Wynter
ON THE DOUBLE

Friday 12th. Two days
John Payne . Mary Murphy
HELL'S ISLAND (TECH.)

Ann Sheridan . Steve Cochrane
COME NEXT SPRING (TECH.)

Monday 15th. Two days
Betty Hutton . Cornel Wilde (TECH.)
THE GREATEST SHOW ON EARTH

Wednesday 17th. Two days
Gregory Peck . Helen Westcott
THE GUNFIGHTER

Cameron Mitchell . Lee J. Cobb
GORILLA AT LARGE

Friday 19th. Two days
Jerry Lewis . Helen Traubel
THE LADIES' MAN (TECH.)

Gordon Jackson . Christina Gregg
TWO WIVES AT ONE WEDDING

Monday 22nd. Two days
Robert Mitchum . Eleanor Parker
HOME FROM THE HILL

Wednesday 24th. Two days
Doris Day . Howard Keel
CALAMITY JANE
The Bowery Boys
IN THE MONEY

Friday 26th. Two days
Tony Randall . Eddie Hodges
Archie Moore — ADVENTURES OF
HUCKLEBERRY FINN

Monday 29th. Two days
Hayley Mills . Jane Wyman
POLLYANNA

Wednesday 31st. Two days
Elizabeth Taylor . Laurence Harvey
Eddie Fisher—BUTTERFIELD 8 (TECH.)

COMING		
ATTRACTIONS	Cimarron	Glenn Ford
FOR	The Great Caruso	Mario Lanza
FEBRUARY	Bells Are Ringing	Dean Martin
	Pure Hells of St. Trinians . .	Cecil Parker
	Two Faces of Dr. Jekyll . .	Paul Massie
	Two Rode Together . .	James Stewart
	The Giant	Steve Reeves
	The Greengage Summer . .	Kenneth More
	Village of the Damned . .	George Sanders
	Watch It Sailor . . .	Dennis Price
	The Time Machine . . .	Rod Taylor

READ THE . . .

HOLYWOOD SPECTATOR

FOR ALL THE LOCAL NEWS

PHONE—BANGOR 1566.

Monday, 1st Aug. *Two days*
Jeff Chandler   Fess Parker
THE JAYHAWKERS (TECH.)
Paul Carpenter   Jean Aubrey
DATE AT MIDNIGHT

Wednesday, 3rd Aug. *Two days*
Doris Day . Jack Lemmon
IT HAPPENED TO JANE (TECH.)
Fred MacMurray
GOOD DAY FOR A HANGING (TECH.)

Friday, 5th Aug. *Two days*
Robert Mitchum   Stanley Baker
THE ANGRY HILLS
Gordon Scott
TARZAN'S FIGHT FOR LIFE

Monday, 8th Aug. *Two days*
Clifton Webb . June Allyson . Van Heflin
Lauren Bacall
A WOMAN'S WORLD (TECH.)

Wednesday, 10th Aug. *Two days*
Stanley Baker   Gordon Jackson
YESTERDAY'S ENEMY
Michael London
THE LEGEND OF TOM DOOLEY

Friday, 12th Aug. *Two days*
Sophia Loren . -Anthony Quinn
HELLER IN TIGHT PINKS (TECH.)

Monday, 15th Aug. (By Request) *Two days*
John Mills . Richard Attenborough
DUNKIRK

Wednesday, 17th Aug. *Two days*
Ian Carmichael   Alastair Sim
LEFT, RIGHT, AND CENTRE
Jack Hawkins . THE INTRUDER

Friday, 19th Aug. *Two days*
John Derek . Diana Lynn
ROGUES OF SHERWOOD FOREST (TECH.)
Burt Lancaster . Gilbert Roland
TEN TALL MEN (TECH.)

Monday, 22nd Aug. *Two days*
Robert Ryan . Harry Belafonte
ODDS AGAINST TOMORROW
Ben Johnson, Jan Harrison . FORT BOWIE

Wed., 24th Aug. (By Request) *Two days*
Steve Reeves . Sylvia Koscina
HERCULES (TECH.)

Friday, 26th Aug. *Two days*
Sophia Loren   Tab Hunter
THAT KIND OF WOMAN
Susan Hayward . Jeff Chandler
THUNDER IN THE SUN

Monday, 29th Aug. *Two days*
Jerry Lewis . Joan Blackman
VISIT TO A SMALL PLANET
THE BIG NIGHT

Wednesday, 31st Aug. *Two days*
David Niven . Shirley MacLaine
ASK ANY GIRL (TECH.)
Richard Boone, Eleanor Parker . LIZZIE

Stars in these films were people like Boris Karloff, Christopher Lee, Béla Lugosi, Vincent Price and Lon Chaney. Other films starred famous performers like Marilyn Monroe, Spencer Tracy, Elizabeth Taylor, Humphrey Bogart, James Stewart and Cary Grant.

Western films brought about a re-enactment when watched by children the following day after school, when those who had seen the film could be seen running about the streets and alleyways with silver-coloured cap guns, and rolls of caps being shot off as though they were free, whilst others had a stick which magically became a rifle. And so it was for children that the film they had watched dictated the next day's games, whether it was pirates, ghosts, robbers or space men.

Some of the wonderful films that came out around the end of the 1950s and the beginning of the 1960s were *Darby 0 'Gill and the Little People*, *Pollyanna* and *The Sign of Zorro*. Others titles of the 1960s included *Lawrence of Arabia*, *Spartacus*, *Cool Hand Luke*, *The Dirty Dozen*, *Goldfinger*, *Mary Poppins*, *True Grit*, *The Birds*, *The Jungle Book*, and so on. Romance and murder films were quite popular, but it was usually the names of the stars that dictated whether a film was going to be popular or not. Feature films usually lasted about one and a half hours. To attract audiences, films with casts of thousands were produced, such as *Ben-Hur*, *The Ten Commandments* and *The Robe*. There were also cultural films that broadened your knowledge of the world. Murder & mystery films were very popular with adults.

When a family film was being shown you could sometimes see whole families arriving to watch the film, stocking up on sweets as they entered the cinema. This happened in particular at Christmas, when children were brought for a treat.

Here is a sample of some of the programmes being shown in Holywood Cinema in 1968–9:

1968

Monday 15th January: days	*El Dorado* (John Wayne); three
Thursday 18th January: three days	*The Long Duel* (Yul Brynner);

Monday 22nd January:

Men
Monday 29th January:
Wednesday 31st January:

1969

Monday 12th May:

Thursday 15th May:

Privilege (Paul Jones)
Support film: *The Intelligence*

ZULU (Stanley Baker)
Triple Cross (Yul Brynner)

Hang 'Em High (Clint Eastwood), with support; three days
Carry On Up the Khyber (Sid James)

One of the cinemas lenses used to project film onto the screen

Monday 19th May:

No Way to Treat a Lady (Rod Steiger)
Support film: *Drop Dead Darling* (Tony Curtis)

Wednesday 21st May: *Nobody Runs Forever* (Rod
                            Steiger)
                            Support film: *Deadly Roulette*
                            (Robert Wagner)
Friday 23rd May: *The Parent Trap* (Hayley Mills)
                            Support film: *A Tiger Walks*
                            (Brian Keith)
Friday 23rd May: (Late-night horror show): *The
                            Mummy*
                            (Doors opened at 10.30pm; no
                            person under 16 admitted.)

CINEMA DECLINE

Slowly the threat of television crept in, with the BBC at first showing black-and-white programmes which were viewed on very small screens. With time, more television sets became available to people, if only to rent, and a greater variety of programmes became available. I can remember my friends and I all descending after school on another friend's house where there was a television, to watch in amazement at this miniature cinema show being viewed from the comfort of someone's own home. The picture was small: screens were around 10 to 12 inches, and very dim, flickering and in black and white. Even then we used to talk about how it would be in the future, and how we would be just like the Americans, having large colour televisions to watch. Eventually, commercial television started, and around 1959 Ulster Television came to the small screen, immediately giving more choice to the public; they could sit in front of a warm fire and, without leaving their house, watch a variety of programmes which came along from different television companies, such as *Tea Time with Tommy*, *Romper Room*, *I Love Lucy*, *Bonanza*, *Dr Kildare*, *Lassie*, *Wagon Train*, *The Kelly Show*, *Coronation Street* and *Sgt. Bilko*.

The cinema was now under severe threat and audiences began to dwindle. Although television sets were short in number, because of the demand a lot of them were brought over from London by dealers, refurbished and hired out – people were afraid to spend money   on buying a television set in case it broke down, so the next best thing was to hire as the repairs would be free if something went wrong. This led to a boom in hire companies. Companies like Check Rentals, Telefusion and Rediffusion became very popular. They rented out televisions from makers such as Ferranti, Murphy, HMV, Bush, Decca and Philips. Quite a few rental televisions had a meter system where you put money in; this gave you so long to watch programmes, but the only problem was if the meter ran out and you had no change to feed it, especially if you were right in the middle of something interesting!

In 1977 a typical 22 inch television could be rented for £9 per month. Colour television was the final straw that changed things and led people away from the cinemas. The cinema industry started to observe the threat as audiences began to dwindle dramatically. Various innovations were tried to stop the decline in audience numbers, such as changing screen and film sizes, putting on late films or stage shows, bringing in Cinemascope, Todd-AO, VistaVision, wide screens, more X-certificate films and 3D films using the red-and-green cardboard glasses to view them. Unfortunately, these ideas were not a great success. Bingo became popular and was tried in many cinemas. For example, the Tonic cinema in Bangor tried bingo sessions, but due to dwindling support had to cease. Alas, it was all in vain and cinemas throughout Northern Ireland, as with everywhere else, came to the point where they had to close their doors, one by one.

The 'Troubles' in Northern Ireland also began to have an impact on the number of cinemagoers and cinemas. In 1977 cinemas in Newtownards, Bangor and Comber were targets for terrorist incendiary bombs, the cinema in Newtownards being completely gutted by fire. Also in the same year the owners of Holywood Cinema decided it might be a good idea and more profitable to change the use of the cinema, as audiences were dwindling. At a meeting of the North Down Borough Council concern was expressed over a proposed conversion of Holywood Cinema.

Holywood Cinema Co. Ltd had applied to convert the cinema at 94–96 High Street to shop, office, warehouse and showroom facilities, and to demolish houses on Downshire Road owned by the cinema to provide a parking area for the offices and shops. Although the Divisional Planning Committee recommended outline permission, the planning committee of the council resolved that the application be deferred and consultations be taken up with the Royal Ulster Constabulary Road Traffic Branch regarding the access of commercial vehicles to the premises. Concern was raised also about the demolition of houses at the bottom of Downshire Road. There was at the time a shortage of housing for those who needed to be re-housed. The Housing Executive were approached to see if there would be any housing available if the scheme went ahead, but the planned changes did not, however, take place.

WHEN THE MOVIES WERE GONE

Eventually, Holywood Cinema got to the sad stage where keeping it open was no longer viable. Television, video tapes, high rates, costs and possibly the new Holywood bypass had all contributed to its demise. At the very final show the projectors were turned off for the last time, the lights extinguished and keys turned in the doors. The large auditorium became just an empty black void, filled with the ghosts and echoes of past laughter, sadness and joy. The cinema waited for its final fate.

After the cinema closed it was put up for sale or to let. It was not long before interested parties came along, although unfortunately not to revive the cinema as such. Carpets were sold for a short time out of the cinema. A snooker club was opened, providing a number of snooker tables, and given the large space available there was plenty of room to surround a table and still have plenty of elbow room to play. The snooker club applied for permission to provide a bar on the premises. There were reports that Holywood Cinema was going to be turned into a supermarket, but one problem with this idea appeared to be the lack of parking.

Seats were removed and the ground floor was converted and levelled for roller skating, skaters careered around merrily to the sound of modern music. At one time a local band also used the building for band practice. Then to everyone's surprise the cinema was eventually turned into a nightclub called The Deep.

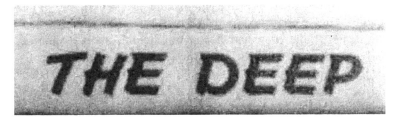

THE DEEP

Before the opening of The Deep nightclub much concern was raised by a number of different bodies and individuals about having something of this nature in the quiet town of Holywood. The council received six letters of complaint, although there were of course people who welcomed the club as somewhere different to go to in the evenings. The Deep was an unlicensed club where people brought their own drink with them, although soft drinks could be bought in the club. It opened until the early hours of the morning.

The Deep nightclub was a very popular, modern, trendy place to go, and inside the music blared loudly as people danced away the night in the vast space of what was once the cinema's auditorium. At the front, hot food could be bought and patrons could book a taxi without having to leave the club.

The owner's idea was to eventually buy numbers 1 and 2 Downshire Road, demolish them and make a car park for the club, and also to eventually turn the old cinema balcony into a restaurant. However, the noise of the music and people coming and going, although popular with those attending, was not too popular with nearby residents. At one point a specialist in air pollution and noise control was brought in and made a lengthy investigation at the club. In his report he said there were two obvious noise outlets: the main entrance doors and the fire escape doors at Downshire Road. The noise was measured at 67dBA.

At a meeting in August 1984, members of North Down Borough Council were informed that the planning department were preparing enforcement notices against the proprietors of The Deep nightclub. They were urged by the council to act as quickly as possible as residents of the area had been complaining about a number of disturbances caused (they believed) by people leaving or entering the club, fights and general noise from the club, although whether all this could be attributed to patrons of The Deep is debatable. The council was informed that a warning letter had already been sent to the club. However, other events were set to alter the future of The Deep.

At around 2.45am on the morning of 16th December 1984 a 60 pound terrorist bomb exploded outside the nightclub. It was full of nuts and bolts which shattered windows in a nearby housing development. It was believed that the bomb was aimed at off-duty police and army personnel who frequented the club. The bomb did not go off at the time set, however, and because it was such a wet night everyone had left the club early, which meant no one was injured although damage was caused to the surrounding property. After this The Deep nightclub closed down, once more leaving the future of the cinema up to fate.

CHANGES

Unlike some cinemas that survived the cinema recession and eventually came back to life as a multiplexes complete with surround sound, large screens and luxury seats, this did not happen in Holywood. With multiplex cinemas the idea was that a number of films could be shown at the same time; if one film did not make money perhaps the others would. The problem in adopting this approach was the cost of the extra equipment and the building renovations, even if the cinema was large enough to be altered in this way.

In 1994 the only surviving cinema building left in Holywood was demolished brick by brick and carted away for dumping. What was once a place of laughter, tears and joy became a vacant space, until eventually a modern building combining shops and offices was built upon the site.

As with most things, we never really appreciate them fully until they are gone forever. When black-and-white and then colour television started to become more common and affordable, the idea of going out into the cold and wet to see a film was not as attractive as sitting by a warm cosy fire at home, watching a variety of programmes and films in comfort, even though the televisions were not large-screen sets and local programmes finished at around 10.30pm every night. Cinemas started to dwindle, not only in Belfast but throughout the country until eventually your choice was limited or you needed to travel to find a suitable cinema.

Things progressed and soon black-and-white television started to become tiresome as the colour television that was now available came to the fore, along with home video machines and a variety of films on video. So, home videos took off and provided television viewers with even more entertainment. Eventually, however, the novelty of colour television/videos wore off and people started to slowly return to the cinemas that were left or had been rebuilt as multiplexes. Unfortunately for Holywood, though, its cinema was no longer there.

Film used to arrive at cinemas on a number of reels. This then changed to the complete film on one reel, then digital projectors with film being projected with a digital projector instead of the old type of film projector. Over the years cinemas have changed so much. As well as their function of showing films, some have cafes and restaurants in them, selling food. From what was termed (by some people, for some cinemas) 'the fleapit' to the new multiplex cinemas of today, design, seating, comfort, viewing and sound have all been updated to reflect what is now expected as the required standard.

If a cinemagoer was to travel through time from one of the first silent film cinemas to see today's cinemas they would gasp in amazement at the changes – the surround sound, the comfort – and find it awesome to gaze at the ultimate cinema experience: the IMAX cinema screen in modern 3D. Some films are even accompanied by appropriate smells, wind effects and moving seats – the 4D experience! Modern cinemas are hopefully here to stay, with comfort and technology all improving to help them stay in business.

If you want to step back in time, thankfully there are still some nostalgic private cinemas in existence such as those owned by brothers Noel and Roy Spence: the Tudor and the Excelsior – Art Deco vintage cinemas in Comber. Faithfully and lovingly created, like time capsules, they transport you back in time to when cinemas were in their heyday.

Alas, with Holywood Cinema gone, now only the memories remain; those memories only being related by those who had the experience of being there. The younger generation of today have missed that experience, but they will eventually have memories and experiences of their own to pass on.

Holywood Cinema during demolition

Demolition of the cinema

THE TONIC

Throughout the years, if you had enough money, you would take the train to the Tonic cinema in Bangor and watch the latest blockbuster films being shown, which were not being shown in Holywood. Many travelled from Holywood to Bangor to spend a few hours in what was classed as a luxury cinema. It was an Art Deco building, and such a wonderful cinema that it's worth saying a few words about its history.

It was a landmark building, and its architect, John McBride Neill, was responsible for designing other cinemas in Ulster around the time the Tonic was built. It opened its doors on 6th July 1936   and had a seating capacity of over 2,000, but still the crowd was so big at the opening that hundreds were turned away. Viscount Bangor headed the ceremony, and inside a band of the Welch Regiment announced the opening with a fanfare of trumpets and drums. Harry Winfield played the mighty Compton theatre organ, and the first film to be shown was *The Man Who Broke the Bank of Monte Carlo*, starring Ronald Colman.

The cinema was massive, arguably the largest in Northern Ireland at that time, and very luxurious, which made it quite a treat to visit every so often. In 1957 the Tonic celebrated Pinewood Studios' 21st anniversary by showing six films that were made at Pinewood. The Tonic was closed for extensive renovations in 1969, and when it reopened to the John Wayne film *Hellfighters* on 3rd March it was renamed the Odeon. To locals, however, it would still be known as the Tonic, and when Belfast Cinemas took ownership in 1975 the name was restored.

As the number of cinemas declined, the Tonic suffered the same fate in loss of customers and revenue. At one time plans were put in for a licensed restaurant but were turned down, as was a request to have a seven-day cinematograph licence, all to help draw in patrons. Other applications for changes of use consisted of one for a supermarket and another for a retail furniture shop with showroom. In 1983 the last film was projected onto the Tonic's large screen. This made way for a period in which the building was used as a bingo hall, which also failed to attract the crowds.

The building eventually closed and became vacant, and in 1984 was offered to the North Down Borough Council for an annual rental. At one time the council had considered using the cinema as a civic centre; however, they turned the offer down. Unfortunately, over a period of time the cinema was then vandalized and fell into disrepair before being destroyed by a fire in 1992. The ground was sold and a number of elderly people's residences now stand in its place.

OTHER VANISHED BUILDINGS/BUSINESESS

As with Holywood's cinema, over the years various buildings including houses as well as small shops and businesses have disappeared; for some the owners retired, for others the buildings have been demolished. Some of them were well-known public locations; others, such as private houses, unless architecturally pleasing are usually only remembered by those who occupied them. But as we look back we realize that although at the time a building disappearing may not have seemed important, and indeed some had to be demolished for reasons of safety and progress, another piece of Holywood's history was disappearing for good; part of the fiber of the town. Such is progress.

When people look at a building they see it how it stands at that particular moment in time and its present purpose; that same building, however, may have been built for a completely different reason and changed its purpose over the years to accommodate changing requirements. This gives it a history. A building that is now a warehouse may have started its existence as a bank, then a hotel, and so on, becoming a part of numerous different people's lives. When looking at old buildings, it's well worth thinking about the different generations of people who have been involved with the place over the years, and how it affected their lives. Modernization and progress will always happen, but we should sometimes consider that there are numerous buildings of historical, human and architectural interest that can be utilized and updated, without having to demolish them.

Here are a few buildings and businesses in the town that have disappeared or nearly disappeared for one reason or another; some you may remember, others not. A few have been demolished or closed fairly recently and are now a part of our local history, never to be seen again.

After the fire

Gone: the Strathearn Hotel

In October 1977 the Strathearn Hotel, formerly Loughview Hotel, burnt to the ground. This was a large hotel situated on the main Belfast Road with a beautiful view over Belfast Lough. Popular for meals and drinks, during the week the hotel hosted a Country and Western night, and there was a popular disco which was a favorite with locals and people from Belfast. Entertainment in the hotel changed weekly; a sample programme from October 1976 runs as follows:

- Thursday 21st: Ruby Murray (in lounge); Wagon Wheel Club; Pat Ely and Rocky Tops. Dancing 8.30pm–1.00am.

- Friday 22nd: Ruby Murray; Maxims Country & Western; Dave Lee and the Show Stoppers.

- Saturday 23rd: Ruby Murray; Cheek Cheekies Dancing Club to the Fabulous Playboys.

- Monday 25th: Stardust Super Disco.

- Tuesday 26th: Grand Cabaret with comedian Tom Raymond.

- Wednesday 27th: Good Time Charlie's Disco.

In 1975 plans for a car park extension and leisure centre, which would have included a swimming pool, gymnasium, squash court and sauna, were put before North Down Borough Council. However, there was much concern already about the behavior of some of the patrons, so the plans were deferred to seek comments from neighboring residents. In October 1977 at around 4.00am a chef who was on night security duties discovered a fire which had started in the main function room. The alarm was raised and the four guests and three members of staff who were present in the building escaped unharmed. Brigades from Holywood, Bangor and Belfast rushed to the scene but the hotel was totally ruined within an hour. It was unknown what started the fire at the time; the owners vowed to rebuild the hotel, but as time went by the ground was cleared of rubble and the site eventually ended up having houses built upon it.

Gone: Warwick's

Warwick's hardware store at the bottom of Shore Street was for years a popular shop for the do-it-yourself fanatic; it was a lot handier to call in there for supplies than to travel to Belfast for them. Unfortunately, the large national do-it-yourself chain stores started to sprout up, making competition hard for the smaller retailer. When Warwick's was trading they also had their own building section, carrying out building work and repairs to houses, offices, etc. throughout Holywood and further afield. At the rear of the shop there was a large shed full of bricks, sand, cement, sections of fencing and building supplies. There was also a wood supply where you were able to purchase and get cut various lengths of timber. A large circular saw zipped and ripped through planks and boards, cutting them to the precise size you required. The shop always provided a good customer service with plenty of help for the aspiring handyman.

71

Gone: shops in Patton's Lane

Coming off the main street into Patton's Lane, you were always amazed by the variety of little shops tucked away in that small area. In the 1960s, among other establishments, there used to be a wonderful antiques shop in Patton's Lane. This was an Aladdin's cave of items that kept you mesmerized whilst trawling through it. As well as the usual antiques such as paintings and vases, there were various other items such as antique guns, old fishing nets, glass balls used for floats and rusted cannons retrieved from the bottom of the sea along with their cannonballs. Other businesses in Patton's Lane over the years included a taxi depot, hairdressers and bookies, among others. In 1986 the lane got a makeover, but sadly over time the shops became vacant and eventually were knocked down.

Gone: Elliotts, sweet shop

This was where Elliotts was situated, at the bottom of Downshire Road. It had a great variety of sweets, lemonade and ice cream. It was a favorite with locals, particularly if heading to watch a show at the cinema.

Gone: horse trough

Horses used to stop here for a well-earned drink outside the Old Priory Church.

Gone: doctor and dental surgeries

At one time the dental surgery of Mr Eric Hayes operated from the other half of this house, before its demolition. Before him the surgery was occupied by Mr Calvert who had moved his practice from St Helens, across the road. The part of the building that is left was once a doctor's surgery belonging to the Dr Blair Practice; eventually it moved and became part of the Priory Surgery beside *Johnny the Jig*.

NSU Quickly auto cycles were being advertised for £62/10/0
Excursions from Holywood to Dublin 1st class 31/6   2nd class 22/-
Polaroid cameras were on sale in Norwoods Pharmacy for £9/19/6

These photographs show Spencer Street in the process of being demolished. At the rear of this was Hill Street; both streets consisted of rows of terraced houses. At the top of Hill Street, outside the school, one house operated a small shop selling sweets to the local children; there was also a shop around the corner in Spencer Street which changed hands and eventually belonged to a Scottish gentleman, Mr Binnie. This was a favorite with everyone in the area as the shop carried quite a variety of groceries and sweets.

Holywood Cricket Club before demolition

Gone: house in Redburn Square

In this photograph we see Redburn Square. Upon demolition of the white house on the right-hand side, a new building belonging to the Fold organization was built in its place. At one time in the rear garden of the house there was an interesting feature which appeared to be the remains of an old Belfast tram.

Gone: the old railway station

Looking towards Redburn Square from Hibernia Street outside what would have been Rosamond Praeger's art studio, we can see part of the old Holywood railway station and the stationmaster's house. Unfortunately, the station was badly burnt in a fire.

Gone: Grainger Bros.

(Photo: Courtesy of the *County Down Spectator*)

Situated in Redburn Square/Sullivan Place was the Grainer Brothers building.

Grainger Brothers Services has been part of Holywood for a long time, their impressive office building was a part of Redburn Square for many years.

<u>Gone: the council yard</u>

Holywood council yard at the bottom of Sullivan Place at the rear of Grainger Brothers. A newer council yard has since been built, and the Queens Hall car park now stands where the building was once located.

81

Gone: Reids

Reid's shop, run by two brothers, Ian and Gordon Bossence, was a part of Holywood for over 50 years. Every year, schoolchildren and their parents would head to Reid's for their school uniforms; the brothers were always helpful and full of jokes. The shop carried a great range of clothing, wet gear and shoes.

Gone: Moffett's

Here we see what used to be Moffett's, the butchers at the bottom of Downshire Road. When in use it was quite popular with the surrounding population as a place to buy meat and vegetables of all sorts. Inside you could see large pieces of meat hanging on hooks ready to be cut up into the relevant portions. The shop floor was covered with sawdust and, as the butchers chopped lumps of meat with cleavers on a large wooden block, a never-ending flow of housewives would be queuing up for something for the evening dinner. As you entered the shop, the counter to the left served the meat and on the right an assortment of fresh vegetables sat in colourful rows.

Gone: Richards, electrical shop

Richards, an electrical shop situated on the High Street, was run for many years by well-known Holywood man Ralph Richards.

Gone: High Street shops
Premises that stood here on the High Street were demolished in January 2007. Holywood Pizza Company occupied one building; the other belonged to Marlow Cleaners.

Gone: the Seaside Tavern

In March 2007 a very well-known Holywood pub, the Seaside Tavern, which was situated at Stewart's Place, was demolished. This was a favorite haunt over the years for a large number of locals. It was nestled beside the railway arch. In the summer, trippers going to or from the shore would nip in for a drink to cool them down or for a bite to eat, whilst in winter it was somewhere to warm up as they passed when going to or from the shore.

Nearly gone: St Colmcille's Church

In August 1989 a fire broke out in St Colmcille's Catholic Church at the bottom of My Lady's Mile. This resulted in total destruction of the roof and interior. Services were moved to a temporary location whilst the main body of the church was rebuilt in a more modern design, using some stone from the original building. The tower and spire, although smoke and heat damaged, survived and after careful restoration the church now stands overlooking the town, the old and the new alongside each other.

Nearly gone: the Olde Priory Inn

The Olde Priory Inn has stood for many years and features in many photographs of the town. It was originally called The Belfast Bar. With the Old Priory and graveyard just a short distance away, the inn blends in with the atmosphere and adds character to the town. For many years it provided entertainment and service to Holywood's population; as well as the pub itself serving alcohol and food, the Olde Priory Inn has hosted wedding receptions, parties, entertainment, quizzes and talent competitions, and had a steady band of loyal customers who could be seen there on a regular basis. In years gone by part of the building, which has since been demolished, was used as a Wesleyan chapel where Methodists paid £7 a year as rent. The door which connected the room to the bar was boarded up, and part of the inn later became the first art studio of Rosamond Praeger. Through the years it has also been used as a ballroom and Girl Guide hall. In the 1940s it suffered fire damage and was refurbished.

Gone: these two impressive houses stood on the Church Road

Gone recently: Herron's shop

Herron's shop on the Church Road closed its doors in 2016 after serving thousands of customers for over 40 years. The shop sold a variety of goods such as newspapers, sweets, groceries and tobacco, and every year a small forest appeared outside the shop as the area was taken over with Christmas trees for sale. It is another landmark shop that will be sadly missed.

That was just a very small selection of some of the buildings and businesses that have disappeared or nearly disappeared from Holywood over the years, and no doubt there will be many more. When walking around Holywood one can see continuous changes taking place as buildings are renovated or demolished. New buildings are being built but when looking along the main street it is interesting to note the purpose of most buildings has changed but most have remained the same as far as structure is concerned.

In the past as well as there being a number of substantial large buildings in Holywood there were also quite a few working garages in the town which also served petrol. In plentiful also were a great variety of pubs for those that liked a little tipple. One did not have to stagger too far before coming across a different one.

Today in this modern age quite a few buildings, although of unchanged structure have been changed into cafes selling coffee. On a good day you will see numerous people sitting outside them at tables sipping their coffee, chatting and watching Holywood go about its business.

Let's travel back in time now and have a look at a small selection of some of the trader's local advertisements in the past as well as some snippets of news from various years.

RAILWAY INN, HOLYWOOD

BIG FREE DRAWS

THIS SATURDAY NIGHT, 23rd DECEMBER

Free tickets given out all day Saturday, also
Saturday night

COMMENCING EARLY NEW YEAR

BAR MEALS

Good parking

We wish all our Customers
A HAPPY CHRISTMAS AND
A BRIGHT NEW YEAR

NORMAN AND JOAN CARMICHAEL

Licensed Restaurant

LUNCHES
Available 12.30 p.m. — 2.00 p.m.

DINNER
from 7.00 p.m. — 10.00 p.m.

(CLOSED DECEMBER 25th, 26th and 27th)

**30 HIGH STREET, HOLYWOOD,
CO. DOWN
Tel: 5880 and 4398**

Proprietors: Raymond & Anne McClelland

91

TOG'S ICES

95

Holywood Road Safety Committee is presenting a
Special New Year Film Show in

THE QUEEN'S HALL

SULLIVAN PLACE. HOLYWOOD

THURSDAY, 18 JANUARY, 1973

at 7.45 p.m.

Films to be shown are New and in Full Colour.
They include:

★ DESTINATION VIENNA — A delightful travelogue featuring a journey by car through Austria to Vienna.

★ THIS TIME TO-MORROW — A dramatic and gripping profile of the Le-Mans 24 hour race.

★ A CITY FOR ALL SEASONS — London throughout the year. A sparkling colour portrait all woven into a resplendant tapestry to the music of Sir Edward Elgar.

★ SAFE AND SOUND — A highly entertaining film featuring Paddy Hopkirk giving advice on driving.

ADULTS ONLY — ADMISSION FREE

COME ALONG AND AND BRING YOUR FRIENDS

NEWS AND TRIVIA

1835

- Thomas Greg from Holywood brought back an Egyptian mummy from Thebes (Luxor) in Egypt. This is now one of the most popular attractions in the Ulster Museum. The mummy, a woman, was known as Kabooti, the daughter of a priest of Amun. We now know her as Takabuti. He presented the mummy to the Belfast Natural History Society and in 1835, in front of around 130 gentlemen, the mummy was unwrapped. The mummy dates from the 7th century BC.

1870

- Holywood had a coastguard station at the Kinnegar.
- Some taxi cab fares:
  - From the railway station, Post Office or maypole to Marino or Farmhill Road = 1s.
  - From above to Sydenham Post Office or Glencraig church = 2s.
  - Fares between 10.30pm and 6.00am charged at double the fare.
- Porter luggage fares for carrying boxes/trunks in the Holywood area = 2d.
- Anyone not bathing in the proper bathing places could be liable to a fine of up to 40s.

1875

- Someone carried out an experiment for a full year and discovered that the climate of Holywood was 2 degrees warmer than that of Belfast.
- A meeting was held in the Town Hall regarding the extension of Holywood Waterworks to take in areas such as Knocknagoney, Ballymenoch and Craigivad. Objections were raised as this could lead to an increase in rates, and the notion was turned down.

- Holywood Cricket Club was officially founded, although it is thought a cricket club may have been unofficially established before this date.

1888

- In July a small disturbance broke out in Holywood that involved soldiers who were stationed at Kinnegar. The fighting started after the soldiers, who had had a little too much to drink, came out of a pub in the High Street. Fighting broke out between some of the soldiers and members of the local constabulary, who were trying to quell their high spirits. Civilians then joined the fracas and the soldiers started throwing stones, breaking windows and wrecking whatever they could get their hands on. Further soldiers who had been sent to calm the situation also became involved in the fighting. This continued until a further picket was sent from the Palace Barracks and reinforcements from the constabulary brought the situation under control.

1889

- Off Holywood in the Belfast Lough stood a manned lighthouse on platforms to help guide ships through the channel, this was before unmanned buoys. As well as having a light it also had a large weather vane and a bell that could be used to warn ships in the case of dense fog. On a foggy day in March the paddle steamer *Earl of Ulster* was heading past near Holywood when suddenly it somehow lost its course in the fog as it passed the Holywood Bank Lighthouse. One of the paddle boxes collided with the lighthouse pillars which supported it, and part of the structure was knocked down into the sea along with the lighthouse keeper Robert McLean. A boat had to be lowered to rescue him.
- A terrible tragedy happened on the railway near Dee Street Bridge where the Bangor to Belfast train had stopped. There was poor visibility when the 07.40 rail car from Holywood ran

into the rear of it killing 18 people and injuring many more.

1892

- Dunvilles Old Irish Whiskey was recommended by the medical profession in preference to French brandy.
- In the 1890s the Kinnegar had its own golf club.
- At Holywood sessions a man was charged with stealing flowers from a garden at Sydenham. In his statement the defendant said that when passing the garden he reached over the hedge and picked a rose. He was ordered to pay 10s and costs.

1897

- Police were investigating a robbery that took place at the Kinnegar Bar. A box containing around £57 was stolen.
- The Railway Hotel went on sale by auction, the entire contents to be sold.
- Cultra Sailing Club was represented on the Clyde by a number of local boats.

1898

- At a meeting of Holywood Town Commissioners, payment of monthly accounts was discussed and cheques were raised in respect of:

  Sanitary account: £7.6s.2d
  Waterworks: £21.12s.5d
  Cemetery: £12.11s.5d
  Gas lighting for street lamps: £5

- A letter was received from Mr McClelland, captain of the local fire brigade, appointing a James Savage Jr to fill a vacancy in the fire service. The terrible state of Byron Street in the Kinnegar was also discussed, and it was suggested that a Mr Allen should consult the owners of houses on the street to

99

see if they would put the road in order.

- In August two men were unfortunately drowned in Belfast Lough. One of them was a former boatman at Cultra; the other a coachman who was employed by Mr G. Dunville of Redburn.

- Snow could be found on a more regular basis at this time, leading to Holywood having its own tobogganing club. The captain was Richard Patterson, the hon. secretary was J. Barrett and there were 25 field stewards.

1901

- Some local businesses:

The Belfast Hotel
The Kinnegar Hotel
Mrs Abraham, tobacconist
R. Boyd, grocer
Mrs Bell, grocer
G. Brennan, barber
Miss Burns, dressmaker
Robert Ferris, builder
R Galway, butcher
Phoenix Fire Office
G. Watson, bootmaker
The Seaside Tavern
D. Magee, confectioner
W. Donnan, watchmaker
P. Lennon, fruiterer
Sun Fire & Life, office
Crighton Livery Stables
Belfast Banking Company
Cyclist Arms Hotel

- During the day trains ran every hour, and every half hour in the morning and evening for commuters. They ran from 6.30am until 11.00pm.

- Holywood Post Office had an express telegraph office which was open throughout the week and also on a Sunday from 9.00am–10.00am. These were the days when the telegram was the quick way to send a message, usually being delivered by a uniformed motorcyclist.

- There were five Temperance Societies in Holywood at this time.

1904

- There were now six Temperance Societies in Holywood.

- The population of Holywood was around 3,840.

- The Royal Irish Constabulary Barracks in Holywood consisted of a sergeant – Sergeant Donaldson – and seven constables.

- Holywood schools consisted of:
  - Sullivan Upper
  - Sullivan National
  - Parochial National Schools
  - National School (RC)
  - Select Schools, Church Road

- Holywood Urban District Council held their meetings in the Town Hall, which was lit by gas and contained a raised platform for concerts that could accommodate around 500 people. It also housed a newsroom, chess room and public library.

- The Post Office had mail deliveries at 7.30am, 10.30am and 3.45pm.

1910

- Some institutions in Holywood at this time:

Northern Banking Co.

Holywood Gas Co.
Holywood Golf Club
RNI Yacht Club
Holywood Cricket & Tennis Club
Holywood Air Gun Club
Holywood YMCA
Holywood Masonic Lodge
Ulster Rifle Association
Holywood Orange Institution
Holywood Gymnastic Club
Holywood Newsroom
1st Holywood Troop Boy Scouts
Temperance Societies

- The local RIC barracks contained a sergeant and four constables.

- Plans were produced for the construction of an electric tramway travelling from Belfast to Holywood, but unfortunately it did not materialise.

1911

- In April of this year, at a meeting of Holywood Urban District Council, permission for steam-rolling to be carried out and the purchase of 200 tones of Newry stone for the main road was given. At the same meeting Dr Donnan reported that the general health of Holywood residents was good, but that there had been one fatality from diphtheria.

- Advertisements offered free passages to Australia for those wanting to work as laborers in the sugar plantations. Wages were 25s per week.

- A list of names were taken by the police regarding local Kinnegar inhabitants being subjected to boys who were not supplied with proper bathing boxes and bathing attire bathing in the sea opposite their houses. No proceedings were taken on the matter.

1912

- Some local businesses:
  Mr Bell, grocer
  Mary Gilpin, confectioner
  R. McConnell, chimney sweep
  Rbt Curley, pawnbroker
  William Berry, blacksmith
  J. Wright, bootmaker
- Holywood Fire Station was run by Captain W. Gavin; he had seven firemen under his control.
- Holywood had a golf club, cricket and lawn tennis club, air gun club, cage bird society, rifle association, scout troop and a working men's club.

1914

- At a meeting of Holywood Urban Council the bank book showed a credit balance of £9.9s.11d. Monthly accounts of £143.14s.5d were passed for payment and included salaries of officials.
- The secretary of the Holywood Working Men's Club asked whether the council had decided to hold the town court in the Town Hall or in the King Edward VII Memorial Hall. The town clerk said they were waiting for the County Council who had done nothing definite as yet.

1917

- In February a whist drive took place at the Military Convalescent Hospital in Holywood, and 70 patients and their relations spent a most enjoyable evening. There were a number of prizes provided and tea, light refreshments and cigarettes were distributed.
- In August the 1st Holywood Troop Boy Scouts marched, headed by their bugle band and with colours flying, to Cultra to visit Cultra Manor, residence of their president, Sir Robert J. Kennedy, to present him with the challenge flag won by them in

competition with other teams. After speeches and tea the troop gave displays of Morse signaling and physical drill. They then returned to Holywood, led by the band.

- In 1917 the following cinemas were showing films in Belfast:

The Royal Cinema, Arthur Square
Duncairn Picture Theatre
Alhambra
Willowfield Picture House
Clonard Kinema House (adjoining Gt Northern Railway)
New York Cinema, York Street
Kelvin Picture Palace
Lyceum Cinema
Imperial Corn Market
Panopticon, High Street

1918

- Some local businesses:
E. Abraham, tobacconist
Mrs Broderick, confectioner
Grainger Bros., contractors
Northern Banking Co.
Holywood Gas Co.
J. Meneely, auto engineer
W. Copeland, grocer
M. Ellis, spirit merchant
Sweeny,   chemist
Unit Construction
A. Anderson, clothier
H. Donaldson, tailor
W. Kennedy, chemist
White Star Inn
Kearney Bros., outfitters
Rbt Aiken, grocer
Edward Hill, newsagent
Lennox, grocer
Kinnegar Service Station
J. Foster, grocer

- A petty session's court started and was held regularly in the King Edward VII Memorial Hall.
- Also, in the same hall a social and dance was held for local soldiers. Over 200 soldiers and their lady friends sat down to tea and fruit, and were also supplied with cigarettes. Afterwards, dancing took place with music supplied by Morris Rainey (piano) and J. Campbell (violin). Everyone remarked on how much they enjoyed themselves.
- At a meeting of the Urban District Council it was resolved that the surveyor's plan (with an estimate of £10) for repair of the Kinnegar would go ahead. Notices were to be addressed to owners of property in the Kinnegar.
- When a party of soldiers were engaged in bombing practice at Holywood in July one of the bombs, after being thrown, struck a parapet and rolled back into the bay. Lieutenant Knapp picked up the bomb with the intention of throwing it back but it exploded as it was thrown. Knapp and Private Legoe were seriously wounded but made satisfactory progress after being taken to hospital.

1920

- Some prices at this time:

  Cherry Blossom boot polish = 1s.2d
  Marvello the Wizard Washing Wonder
  (no steeping; no rubbing) = 6d
  Day old chicks = £1 per dozen
  Hatching eggs = 10s per setting

1921

- Some local businesses:
  Mrs Aiken, grocer
  T. Dunwoody, coal merchant
  R. Milligan, nurseryman/florist
  R. Neill, coal merchant
  The Maypole Hotel
  Mrs Clarke, confectioner
  The Seaside Tavern
  H. Donaldson, tailor
  R. Herron, fruit merchant
  Mawhinney, cabinetmaker
  Holywood Gas Co.
  J. M. Kelvey, cycle agent
  Grainger Bros., contractors

Northern Banking Co.

J. McKenna, tobacconist

- Royal Mail deliveries took place in Holywood at 7.30am, 11.30am and 3.45pm. Outgoing mail was despatched at 7.45am, 2.20pm and 6.20pm.
- Holywood fire station was situated at the Town Hall. The captain of the brigade was Charles Gavin from Spencer Street and his lieutenant was James Savage from Strand Street.
- In April a new magistrate was appointed to the Commission of the Peace for County Down. He was Thomas H. Keown, who was originally from Killyleagh. He took up the position and adjudicated at Holywood and Newtownbreda petty sessions.
- In July of this year a prompt rescue saved the life of a Holywood boy who was four years old. He was rescued by John Mulholland from Belfast when he overbalanced whilst playing on top of a pier and fell into the water. He was being swept out to sea by the tide when he was rescued.
- In September 1921 the First Holywood Presbyterian Church in Bangor Road, which had been closed for almost two years whilst undergoing extensive repairs and renovation, was reopened and rededicated. The preacher was the Rev. Dr Purves of Elmwood, and the congregation raised over £3,500 towards the cost of repairs, with a debt of £2,000 remaining. In 1975 the church was to be the target of vandals, with damage being done to some stained glass windows.

1922

- Triumph motorcycles were on sale in Holywood, costing   from £65–£155. Triumph pedal cycles cost £12–£20.

1924

- A dance was held in the Working Men's Club to celebrate winning Orme Billiard League & Single Hand Championship. Prizes were presented by Messrs Nelson Trimble and T. Johnston.
- A wireless crystal radio set was being sold for £1.6s.6d.

- At a Holywood Council meeting tenders were submitted for the supply of new equipment for the fire brigade.

- At Cultra Manor in Sir Robert Kennedy's estate, a fox cub was shot dead by the gamekeeper. One shot at a distance killed it. It was thought to be most unusual at the time for foxes to be active in the area.
- An advert from the time:

ROMOR
Is a fascinating & fatal vermin destroyer
Rats & mice eat it greedily & quickly
die. No failures with **ROMOR** it always
kills Tins 7½

- In August the Boot Shop in the High Street was completely destroyed by fire. A large explosion occurred, blowing out the front of the shop window, and pieces narrowly missed a Bangor bus passing by. Local firemen rushed to the scene and used their one hose to try to put out the fire. Seeing that this was futile, they concentrated on dampening down the Central Hotel situated next door. It was not known how the fire started.

1935

- The petty sessions were held in the King Edward VII Memorial Hall and the town court in the Town Hall.
- A new Hillman Minx saloon could be bought for £159; a Ford Popular for £115; a Wolseley Wasp for £165; and a Fiat Saloon de Luxe for £185. The cost of a Raleigh push bike started from £4.12s.6d.
- Duffy's circus came to town that July, bringing acts such as Pantzer Wonder Midgets plus a programme of equestrian,

vaudeville and specialty acts. Prices of admission were ls.3d, 2s.4d and 3s.6d.

1939

- A charity football match was held on Easter Tuesday in aid of the local nursing society and drew a large crowd.
- A BSA bicycle could be bought for £5.10s or on easy purchase terms.

1940

- 'The Garrison Theatre' in the Town Hall presented a presentation which featured acts such as: Mavelle the wonder girl, Tiny & Tot the dancing dolls and Mickey Maxis miniature circus.
- Surrounding local cinemas at the time included: the Palace, Bangor; the Tonic, Bangor; Adelphi, Bangor; Ritz, Newtownards; Regal, Donaghadee; Picture House, Comber; and the Cinema, Portaferry.
- In December Holywood's Town Hall was badly destroyed by fire. It was a majestic building built in the 1870s and was used for many local events. The fire was spotted in the morning by someone heading to catch a train, and at the same time the caretaker who lived on the premises had to evacuate the building as it filled with smoke and flames. Fire personnel from Holywood and Belfast fought in vain as the building was completely ruined. The fire appeared to have started in the main hall, quickly spreading to the roof and other parts of the building.

1941

- Some local businesses:
  Belfast Co-Operative Society
  J. Gowan, automobile engineer
  E. Hill, grocer
  J. Reid, newsagent
  Turners Fruit Market

S. Orr, chemist
The Seaside Tavern
J. Ballagh & Sons, house furnishers
Downshire Diary
Rockmount Diary
Priory Perk Nursery
Kinnegar Bar
Wilton Bros., funeral furnishers
Isobel's Cake Shop
Cave, confectionery (kiosk in railway station)

- Wednesday was a half day for shops.
- The last census put the town's population at 5,078.
- The RUC station had two sergeants and six constables.
- Some of the various clubs/associations in the town were:
Services Club
Badminton Club
Unionist Club
Yacht Club
Boy Scouts
Golf Club
Cricket and Lawn Tennis Club
Women's Unionist Club
Working Men's Club

- Kearney Bros. opened a new shop in Main Street, Bangor.

1946

- Some local businesses:
The Central Hotel
Belfast Co-Operative Society
Downshire Diary
Priory Park Nursery
J. Reid, newsagent
Turners Fruit Market
Milk Bar & Café
H. Henderson, funeral furnisher
111

J. Ballagh, house furnisher

T. Bell, confectioner

Grainger Brothers, contractors

S. Orr, chemist

Wm Stevenson, painter

The Priory Cycle Depot

Claude Henfrey, ice cream specialist

- On Saturday 25th May a gymkhana and horse jumping competition took place at Ballymenoch Estate. All the best horses and ponies competed for a £200 prize, and £350 was raised for the local forces' Welcome Home Fund. Admission charges were 2s for adults and 1s for children.
- The Austin 10 was being advertised for £270 (8hp) and £330 (10hp); both four- and two-door and in a choice of three colours. An outboard engine for a boat could be bought for £38.
- November 1946 saw the official opening of the Sir Samuel Kelly Memorial Home, gifted by Lady Kelly to the Salvation Army. Situated beside what is now Ballymenoch Park, it eventually became a home for the elderly.

1947

- In July Edward Fossett & Sons Circus came to Holywood, featuring a number of different artists such as the Balasson Troupe, Linley the performing horse, the Georgy Troupe (an aerial ladder act), a troupe of performing monkeys and Bumpa the bucking mule. Admission prices ranged from 1s.9d to 6s.6d.
- Holywood Ratepayers Association met a sub-committee of the Down Regional Education Committee to discuss better facilities for older boys and girls. It was stated that cookery and sewing classes were completely inadequate.
- In December an advertisement appeared for a particular type of dried seaweed which would be bought by agents in Scotland and the South of Ireland. At the time there was an abundance of it on the North Down coast; the advert requested that people

collect it and send it off. There appeared to be a lucrative market for it at the time.

<u>1949</u>

- In 1949 Seapark was officially opened by the then Governor of Northern Ireland, His Excellency Vice Admiral the Earl Granville. It was built at a cost of £20,000 and offered lawn tennis, bowls, hockey, football and putting. It was originally intended to have an outdoor swimming pool but a shortage of labour and materials meant this was deferred. The pavilion when built contained showers, changing rooms, a kitchen and an assembly room.
- Holywood man F.O.W. Bowden (No. 502 Ulster Squadron) won the Royal Auxiliary Air Force inter-squadron race flying a Spitfire at the national air races at Elmdon Airport, Birmingham.
- In October a tender from local firm Grainer Brothers (Ireland) Ltd was provisionally accepted by Bangor Borough Council for the building of an additional reservoir at Ballysallagh at a cost of £155,418.

<u>1951</u>

- The popularity of cinemas at this time can be seen from this list of cinemas in Belfast city alone:

Alhambra
Ambassador
Apollo
Arcadian
Astoria
Broadway
Capital
Castle Cinema
Central Picture Theatre
Cinema
Clonard

113

Coliseum
Crumlin Picture House
Curzon
Diamond Picture House
Duncairn
Forum
Gaiety
Gaumont
Imperial
Lyceum
Majestic
New Princess Palace
Park Cinema
Popular
Regal
Regent
Ritz
Royal
Sandro
Savoy
Shankill
Picturedrome
Stadium
Strand
Troxy

- A gift of around 19 acres of parkland situated at the Bangor side of the town was given to the people of Holywood by Lady Kelly, widow of Sir Samuel Kelly. The council proposed that this be made into a park.

- In May the concluding session of Holywood musical festival took place in Messrs Grainger's Hall. Over 1,000 people attended.

<u>1952</u>

- Some local businesses:

Co-Operative Society
Robert Aiken, grocer
J. B. Cowan, auto engineer
Herron's, grocer
Holywood Upholstery Works
Angus McDonald, antiques
Northern Bank
T. Bell, bakery
A.A. Taxis
T. Bell, restaurant
Fahy's, newsagent
Holywood Cash Stores
Kinnegar Service Station
The Loughview Hotel
Belfast Savings Bank
J. Ballagh & Sons

- Members of the Irish Association of Change Ringers at St Philip and St James church performed a unique peal of bells that was believed not to have been performed before by any ringing association in the British Isles. It comprised 5,024 changes and took three hours and seven minutes to ring.

1953

- This year saw the official opening of the Queens Hall by the Governor of Northern Ireland Lord Wakehurst at a cost of £22,000. Five hundred guests were in attendance. The main contractors were W. Scott & Co., Charles Crichton of Church Road provided the public address system, and the stage and hall curtains were provided by Kearney Bros. Previously, in 1950, at a meeting of Holywood Urban District Council it was announced that a proposal to erect a town hall as part of the Festival of Britain, taking place the following year, had been turned down by the Ministry of Finance.

One Saturday night in the hall saw dancing to Billy Horner and his quintet; admission was 2s.6d. For those attending from outside the town, the last train left for Bangor at 11.29pm and the last Belfast train left at 11.38pm.

- A new Standard 8 car cost £339 plus purchase tax. Pye televisions with automatic picture control were on sale for £64.18s for a 14 inch tube.

1954

- As well as those in Holywood, Bangor, Newtownards and Donaghadee, other cinemas in the County Down area included the Shield Cinema in Ardglass, the Festival Cinema in Crossgar, the Castle Cinema in Dundrum and the Grand in Downpatrick.

- 1954 saw the opening of a number of new buildings, including a new fire station and two schools. In August 1954 Holywood's new fire station opened in Sullivan Place, replacing an old Nissan-type hut that had previously been used. The cost was £12,000. Holywood's new primary school opened, having been built over 17 months at a cost of £73,000 with accommodation for 500 pupils. Holywood Intermediate School also opened its doors this year.

- Ten dogs were poisoned in Holywood over a period of ten days, and the USPCA offered a reward of £20 for information leading to the apprehension of those responsible. A cat was also poisoned, but no definitive connection was found.

- At a meeting of Holywood Urban District Council, Councilor W. E. Russell brought up the matter of gas prices and pointed out that Holywood residents were paying 50% more than Bangor residents. The council decided to send a letter of protest to Belfast Corporation and have the matter addressed.

- The local fire brigade were called to a fire which broke out in a terraced house in Esplanade Terrace in the early hours of the morning. Bangor's fire brigade also attended. The roofs of two houses were gutted but firemen prevented the fire from spreading further.

- At a meeting of Holywood Urban District Council the success of the decision to commemorate the coronation by giving a savings book containing 2s.6d to every child of school age who lived in the town was discussed. This had resulted in the opening of 1,530 gift deposit accounts in the Belfast Savings Bank.

- At an auction, a house and four shops in High Street, Hibernia Street and Gray's Lane were all sold to one local bidder for £1,900.

- In March a meeting was held with Holywood Council, Castlereagh Council and the Hospitals Authority to discuss a plan for setting up a cottage-type hospital on the site of Redburn House. It was the wish of people living in the area to have a hospital in Holywood; the idea was discussed but never came to fruition.

Holywood Horse Show
and Gymkhana Society
ANNUAL
SHOW
will be held on
MAY 21st, 1955
Commencing at 11-30 a.m.

1955

- Some local businesses:

The Loughview Hotel
Belfast Co-Op Society
Crighton Electrical
Leslie Innis, garage
Downshire Diary
Kearney Bros.
L. Innis, Picture House Garage
Kinnegar Filling Station
Belfast Gas Co.
T. Bell, home bakery
Maypole Café
Belfast Savings Bank
A.A. Taxis
Sweeny's Pharmacy
Reid's, drapers
J. Ballagh, house furnisher
Collette Ladies Wear
L. Fahy, tobacconist
Downshire Building Works
G. Brady, spirit merchant
The Old Priory Inn
Ladyneeds, outfitters
Unit Construction
Balmer, provision merchant
Cosy Corner, confectionery
Holywood Upholstery Works
Donaghy Hairdressing
J. B. Cowan, automobile engineer
James Lennox, confectioner
Sallie's Home Bakery

- A new Standard 10 car with push-button door handles and adjustable seats cost £538.10d. The deluxe version cost £580.10s.10d.
- On 17th March Holywood Cricket and Lawn Tennis Club held a grand St Patrick's Night dance in the Queens Hall, with music by Norman Conner and his band. Subscription was 4s and everyone had a great time.
- Buff Bill's Circus came to town in June of this year, for one day. The show featured the death-defying lion tamer Johnnie Keys along with Dawn Desmond, who provided aerial thrills, and sharpshooters Cody and Oran. There were also horses, lions, a bear, baboons and dogs.
- Ards Motorcycle Club held a motorcycle scramble at Ballymenoch, which was televised by the BBC.
- Before the Ulster Folk Museum was established at Cultra, at a meeting of Holywood Urban District Council it was decided to support the proposed venture. Mr Dunne, the chairman, said he understood the idea was that the museum would be established and each town or council would be asked to provide something for the museum. Councilor W. E. Russell said he believed they should support the scheme as there was a lot they could learn from the craftsmen of the past. Councilor Mrs M. A. Smyth said they should go a step further and proposed they make a donation of £10.10s. The council all agreed that they would give any support they could.
- In May Holywood Horse Show & Gymkhana Society held their annual show.
- Holywood Flower Show was held with a variety of flower displays and awards. The show was a great success with a Mr. Mahood from Newtownards winning four firsts.

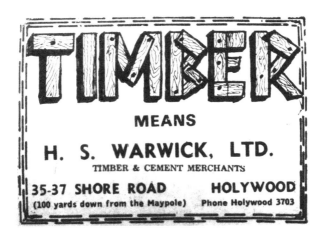

- A Mr. Wilson from Holywood won £505 0s 4d in the Y.P. pools.
- Holywood Urban District Council made a decision to plant trees around the reservoir at Creightons Green. The scheme was to cover 93.51 acres at a cost of £4,114 10s 0d. As well as providing a source of timber for the future and add to the attraction of the reservoir it also helped the unemployment situation.
- Gallagher's cigarettes were on sale for- Med. & Mild-5/5 Tipped- 4/7 for twenty.

1956

- Holywood Urban District Council consisted of the following councillors:

  William Dunne (chairman)
  Dr H. Dorman (vice chairman)
  R. McCorky
  Mrs M. A. Smyth
  Mrs M. Blampied
  R. Dunlop
  F. Gribban
  E. McCavana
  W. E. Russell

- A three-seater Chesterfield suite could be bought for £89. A bedroom suite in mahogany was £79. A Cossor music centre (model 523 'Melody Master') with six-valve 10 inch elliptical speaker, four wavebands (VHF, long, medium and short) and walnut veneered cabinet was £32. A day excursion from Holywood to Dublin by train via Ulster Transport cost 34s return first class and 24s second class (no luggage allowed). At a local hairdresser's, a permanent wave including cutting and styling cost £1. A Milky Way chocolate bar cost 3d.
- According to the manufacturer's guidelines, an Austin A35 achieved 54 miles per gallon at 40mph and 60 miles per gallon at 30mph.

1957

- Holywood Players won the premier award at the Ballymoney Drama Festival with their presentation of *Two Dozen Red Roses*. At Bangor's eleventh annual drama festival they received high praise for their presentation of *The Sacred Flame*.
- There were 249 entries at the Holywood gymkhana and horse show and, although the weather was not great, there was a good attendance.

- Some local prices: Bush radio £16, Waverley cycle £13.19s.6d, hot water bottle 5s.6d, knitting machine £3.12s.5d.
- In August five boats, one of them a mooring boat, sank in the heavy seas at Cultra.

1958

- Mr W. Stevenson from Ballymenoch won the Ploughing Champion of County Down award for the second consecutive year.
- On 8th February the Ulster Group Theatre staged a play in the Queens Hall entitled *Moodie in Manitoba*. On 14th February a grand Valentine's Day ball was held in the hall, with music by Nat Coleman and the Skyrockets.
- In October the BBC programme *Your Questions*, in which members of a local audience put questions to politicians, was broadcast from Holywood.
- Holywood Urban Council again applied to build a small or cottage hospital for Holywood, with 10–20 beds and an emergency section. One idea was to build it at the rear of and opposite the Palace Barracks on the Old Holywood Road.

- At Holywood court 15 motorists were fined following radar speed detections at Dundonald. They were all exceeding the speed limit in a 30mph zone. Fines ranged from £4 to £5.

1959

- Kinnegar Service Station (John Fox) was selling Esso Blue Paraffin at 2s per gallon with free delivery within a 15 mile radius.
- John Ballagh & Sons were selling Parker Knoll fireside chairs for £8.19s.6d, new lawnmowers for £6.10s.1d and grass cutters for £1.1d.
- Kerwoods had on offer a 17 inch Pam television for a £5 deposit followed by 10s weekly payments, reducing to 9s.
- Mr B. Larcher of Holywood entered the Queen's University students' mileage competition and won a brand new Austin A35. He did not have a car at the time (although he had some driving experience) and was obviously delighted!
- Holywood had a ballroom club situated in the Queens Hall. Music was provided by the 6 Men, and there were lessons, competitions and demonstrations. Subs 1s.6d; session fee 3s.6d.

- In April The Not Forgotten Association held a May Queen dance in the Queens Hall. Contestants were asked to apply but the competition was only open to girls living in Holywood and the surrounding district. The prize was to become the May Queen and win a complete evening outfit. Dancing was to Quarternotes.

- In June fire brigades from Holywood, Belfast and Bangor combined to fight some fierce gorse/grass fires on the railway banks at Holywood, near to the railway station. Because of the dry weather, flames spread rapidly out of control and visibility became very poor as the smoke billowed across the railway tracks and surrounding area. At one point firemen had to concentrate their efforts to defend the large gas containers in the gas works as the flames threatened to reach them. The Ordnance

Depot at Kinnegar also gave cause for concern as the flames fanned their way along the embankments. After approximately two hours firemen started to bring the flames under control.

- A public health warning was issued to gypsies encamped at Tillysburn on the Holywood Road. There were originally 100 encamped but that had now reduced to 30

1960

- In May Bangor Borough Council discussed the idea that *Johnny the Jig*, sculpted by the late Rosamond Praeger, could become a symbol of road safety.
- Ten plain Park Drive cigarettes cost 1s.7d.
- In this decade ice lollies and choc ices became very popular.

HOLYWOOD

Undertakers Redundant!

THE HEALTH MAN OPEN ON TUESDAY, 4th JUNE AT 9 a.m.

Jack McClelland 27 Church Road, Holywood

Naturally!

- At Holywood Horse Show, held in Ballymenoch Park, there were 250 entries. There was a top prize of £200 as well as other awards.

- Holywood Players won the Coey Cup at Larne Drama Festival, allowing them to compete in the Northern Ireland one-act finals at Bangor Drama Festival.
- Car tax was £13, but it was to be reduced to £12.10s in 1961.
- Kerwoods were renting 17 inch Pam televisions with polarised screens. They offered free tubes-free indoor aerial-free valves-free service. The cost was £6.10s.0d deposit with 10s weekly payments reducing to 4s.6d.

1961

- In June a large basking shark beached near Seapark, possibly injured by a ship's propeller. It was so badly injured that it was shot dead by soldiers from the Palace Barracks. Health inspectors ordered it to be disposed of so it was cut into pieces and taken to Holywood refuse dump where it was buried under lime.

Basking shark at Seapark
(Photo: Courtesy of the *County Down Spectator*)

- The 3rd Holywood Scout Group held a dance in the Queen's Hall on St Patrick's night, where guests enjoyed dancing to the Norman O'Connor's Band.

- Holywood Players presented *The Ring of Truth* by Wynyard Browne in the Queens Hall.
- The cemetery wall at Priory Corner was lowered, along with gravestones, for safety reasons. Over a period of time, there had been much debate at Holywood Urban District Council about the frequent accidents at this site: as well as it being a bad bend, drivers had difficulty seeing anyone coming around the corner. A crash barrier was also erected on the other side of the road.
- Some television programmes in the 1960s included *Wells Fargo, Perry Como, Watch with Mother, The Flowerpot Men, Whirlybirds* and *Bronco*.

THE SEASIDE TAVERN
THE MOST "IN" INN TO DRINK
IN IN IRELAND!

When ni Holywood please visit the Seaside Tavern where you will receiv ehte utmost in COURTESY, CIVILITY and SERVICE

Proprietors—Ray and Vera Kennedy and Family

Please Note—NO GROUPS, NO GIMMICKS
HOLYWOOD

- Hundreds of personnel took part in a civil defense exercise in North Down, which was held to test our capabilities in the event of a nuclear attack. The scenario was that a two megaton bomb had burst near Holywood. Troops and civilian volunteers made a 5 mile ring around Holywood from Bangor, Conlig, Newtownards, Comber and Dundonald. Rangers and rover scouts acted as casualties. Messages were sent by radio and despatch riders, assuming telephone lines were out of order. In two hours, 96 casualties had been attended to.

<u>1962</u>

- Some local businesses:

> Abbey National Building Society
> Fred Ballagh, fruiterer
> Centra Café
> H. Cromie, hairdresser
> W. Foster, newsagents
> Arcadia Home Bakery
> J. Ballagh, house furniture
> Cosy Corner, confectionery
> L. Fahy, newsagents
> H. Frazer, hardware

- Kerwoods had for sale electric fires from 27s.6d and electric blankets at 50s. TV rental cost a £2 deposit followed by a weekly rental fee of 8s.6d, and it included a free BBC/ITV aerial.
- Driving lessons were advertised at a cost of 10s per lesson in a dual control car. A new Vauxhall Cresta car sold for £918.17s.11d and a new Lambretta scooter cost £139.19s.6d.

127

- In March Holywood's fire brigade were called to a fire at Knocknatten – a 15-roomed thatched house at Cultra. This was a very large and beautiful house with a Norwegian thatched roof. The fire had started in the chimney and then spread to the thatch itself. Holywood Fire Service were first on the scene, but the equipment possessed by the Ulster Unit was inadequate for a fire of this size and so backup was called for. Four units, two from Holywood and two from Bangor, fought the fire for eight hours whilst police, neighbours and AA men rushed to remove furniture from the ground floor. When a length of hose burst and had to be changed the fire flared up, resulting in burning thatch tumbling down and burying some Bangor firemen. They were able to scramble clear and were later treated for minor burns.

Knocknatten
(Photo: Courtesy of the *County Down Spectator*)

- On Saturday 26th May a summer fete was held at Redburn House, which had once been owned by the Dunville family. The opening ceremony was led by Mr Robert McLernon of UTV, and there were model railway rides, displays, sideshows, fancy

128

dress and tours of the house. Admission was 1s for adults and 6d for children. The weather was good and everyone enjoyed themselves.

- The Irish Theatre Ballet of Cork performed new Irish and classical ballet in the Queens Hall.

- Holywood Golf Club was host to the National Association of Groundsmen when they held their first annual field day, displaying different types of turf and grass management equipment.

- Despite the heavy and constant rain we complain about now, in 1962 some concerns were raised about the low levels of water in our local reservoirs. If there was not a substantial rainfall by the end of the year to top them up, it was remarked, the situation would become serious.

- Soldiers from the Sherwood Foresters regiment stationed at the Palace Barracks were caught in the severe snow blizzards which covered the country. They were on exercise in the Sperrin Mountains and nothing was heard from them from Monday until Thursday. The men were glad to get back to the barracks. Some people described the blizzards as the worst in memory, with roads impassable, electricity failing, telephone lines being cut and a shortage of bread and milk all adding to the misery. People on Swain's Hill had to have food delivered by the police and army, and a district nurse set out in an army truck to visit someone at Ballykeel crossroads, but after three hours struggling through the snow had to give up. One fire brought Holywood Fire Brigade, under the charge of fireman Tommy Catherwood, rushing to Meadow Way, a bungalow at Craigivad. A fire had broken out in the roof space, but snowdrifts hindered the fire unit, who became stranded shortly before reaching the bungalow. Lengths of hose had to be run out from the machine to reach the fire. Bangor Fire Brigade attended as backup.

- Although there was no serious problem, a Holywood man was granted permission by the Castlereagh Rural Council to shoot rats at the council's refuse dump at Kinnegar, which was situated across the road from the Palace Barracks.

- Holywood railway station was badly burnt; at around 3.00am a Miss Bussell, who lived adjacent to the station, was awoken by the sound of crackling flames. When she looked out of the window she was amazed to see the railway station on fire, and immediately called the fire brigade. A call for help went out from Holywood Fire Brigade and colleagues from Bangor rushed to the scene to help. Stationmaster William Murtagh escaped the fire but lost most of his belongings; two firemen from Holywood were slightly injured.

- For those who wanted to make their own movies, Norwood Pharmacy was selling a Quartz 8mm cine outfit at £15.17s.6d. This included a pistol grip, two filters, three lenses, a cable release and a pigskin carrying case.

- In October the famous Beatles were booked to play at the King's Hall in Belfast. Admission prices were 20s, 15s, 10s and 7s.6d.

- The Seaside Tavern reopened with a luxurious new lounge for customers.

- Whilst excavating at a building site on the Old Holywood Road, the driver of the excavator uprooted an old tree and found a human skeleton and part of another embedded in the roots of the tree. The skeleton was believed to be more than 300 years old and speculation was that it might have belonged to an Irish chief, Con O'Neil, who died in Holywood. The site was once the location of an old church.

1963

- A lot of debate went on about which authority, Holywood Urban District Council or Castlereagh Council, should receive urban status over Marino, Cultra and Craigivad. It was felt the three areas should come under Holywood Urban District

Council, and after the meeting the council proposed that the Ratepayers Association be notified that the council opposed the bill.

- The board of trustees of the Ulster Folk Museum signed the contract for the conversion of Cultra Manor into a museum.
- The famous singer Frankie Vaughn visited Holywood Youth Club and was given a brief tour. He gave the members words of advice on how to be a good club member and raise funds for the club.

1965

- Holywood Parish Church and friends presented a brand new minibus to the Mission for Seamen. A sum of £700 was raised through collections, subscriptions and coffee mornings. Having the minibus meant that visiting sailors could travel in comfort to many functions.

1966

- At a meeting of the Urban Planning and Development Committee the possible relocation of the maypole was discussed. This idea came from a town plan proposed in 1948, but was reconsidered after numerous complaints from Holywood residents who described the proposal as 'unthinkable' and 'disastrous'.
- In August the Ulster Transport Authority started a new bus route from Holywood to Belfast. This ran via the High Street, Jacksons Road, Old Holywood Road and Knocknagoney, as it does to the present day.
- September brought all the fun of the circus when Duffys Circus came to town.
- After a meeting in the King Edward VII Memorial Hall that around 150 people attended, Holywood householders sent a deputation to the Ministry of Health and Social Services regarding Holywood Urban Council's system of allocating houses.

132

- Holywood's annual regatta had 110 entrants; the evening was rounded off with a dance in the clubhouse.
- Several bowlers from Bangor were using the bowling green at Seapark; they were boycotting the Ward Park green in Bangor because of increased charges by Bangor Borough Council.

```
┌─────────────────────────────────────────┐
│              The Hob                     │
│          RESTAURANT                      │
│      85 HIGH STREET, HOLYWOOD            │
│                FOR                        │
│    MORNING COFFEES, LUNCHES              │
│        AFTERNOON TEAS                     │
│                      FOR THAT             │
│  THE HOB 'HOME MADE' TASTE               │
└─────────────────────────────────────────┘
```

1967

- Some local businesses:

A.A. Taxis
Leonard Fahy, newsagent
J. Orr, butcher
Holywood Boutique
W. Moffett, butcher
R. Richards, electrical
J. Cairnduff, builder
Kinnegar Service Station
T. Bell, bakery
Isobel's Home Bakery
H. Price, upholsterer

133

- Around 70 guests attended a concert at the Tudor Hall, organised by Mr Herbert Dunne in aid of the High Street Presbyterian Church manse fund. This was followed up with an excellent supper.
- Councillors and residents debated new proposals for the Holywood throughpass. Support was mainly for the sea route instead of a route through the town centre. At a council meeting, Councillor W. E. Russell brought up the subject of access to the seafront if the throughpass was built. He had received numerous enquiries from locals about this.
- Work started on the First Holywood (Bangor Road) Presbyterian Church project for the provision of a new lecture hall and car park. The cost, approximately £35,000.
- In this year redevelopment got underway in the Strand redevelopment scheme. The Ministry of Development developed a scheme for creating a pedestrian footpath running all the way from Holywood to Groomsport (approximately 10 miles) at a cost of £10,000. There would be toilets and litter bins at designated spots.
- A day trip from Holywood to Belfast to see the Balmoral show cost 2s.3d by train.
- Holywood's Church of St Phillip and St James featured on the television programme *Songs of Praise*.

- Existing sporting facilities in Holywood at this time were:
  - Schools: one cricket, one football, four hockey, four tennis and two rugby.
  - Local authority: one football, one hockey, three tennis and one bowls.
  - Private: two cricket, one football, one hockey, one Gaelic football and two rugby.
- On one day in January, local firemen had a busy day when they were called to three fires in immediate succession. The first was a fractured gas main which had ignited in the High Street. They were then called to a chimney fire a short distance away; and after this they were summoned to a house fire in Bath Terrace, which resulted in the premises being badly damaged.
- The average house price throughout the UK at this time was £2,530.
- Residents of the Loughview estate complained to the council about parts of the estate having a severe water shortage at the weekends; for some reason, this was happening every weekend. Belfast Water Commissioners were to investigate.
- Holywood Players presented a production in the Queens Hall entitled *Disney & The Witches* with perhaps (at that time) the biggest ever cast. The lead was David McMaster, it was produced by Trevor Hughes and Rowel Friars designed the sets.
- In April Holywood Bowling Club officially opened their green at Seapark. Mr James Savage was welcomed as the new president. The green keeper was Mr Tommy Quinn. Members of the council were present when Mr Savage hoisted the club flag. Mrs McWhinney delivered the first bowl; guests were then invited for tea.
- Some derelict houses in Sullivan Street, High Street and Spencer Street were discussed at the monthly meeting of the council. It was thought these were a danger to children and were being vandalised. The council decided to refer the matter to the town solicitor for advice.

- Residents in Alexandra Park complained about their tap water being badly discoloured – it was described as looking like tea with a sandy substance at the bottom! Samples were taken for chemical analysis.
- Holywood Urban Council decided to approach the War Office with a view to acquiring various properties in the Kinnegar for light industry.
- Loughview Tavern was advertising full board for 10gns per week.
  Bed and breakfast 25s. Lunches from 5s.6d. High teas from 6s6d.

1970

- The council received complaints from the public regarding plastic food containers washing up on the beach. It was believed these may have been thrown overboard from passing ships.
- Kerwoods had three-channel 19 inch televisions available for rental at 10s a week.

1971

- In January there was a general postal strike, meaning no mail deliveries around the Holywood area.
- Holywood fire brigade, along with Bangor, Newtownards and Belfast, fought one of the biggest fires since the war at a timber yard in Duncrue Street.
- The Divisional Public Health Inspector highlighted to council members that Redburn House, built by the Dunvilles, was structurally unsound and might collapse. It had lain derelict for some time and lead had been stolen from the roof; therefore, rainwater had seeped in and the timbers were rotten. It was estimated that the cost of repair would be too much, and the Ministry of Development had shown an interest in using the land for a park; however, the Urban District Council could not determine the precise area of land the council owned as maps seemed to disagree. The town surveyor was to investigate, and it was agreed that some plots of land would be transferred to

136

neighbouring householders to tidy up the border areas before the site was turned into a park. Over a period of time, various fires broke out in the house, interspersed with episodes of vandalism taking place; in December there were three fires in three days!

- Tenants of the Loughview estate had great problems with their electrical voltage supply being very low. EBNI started an investigation.
- Holywood councillors expressed concern about the grey-and-green colour scheme for the new NI Housing development at the Strand.
- Holidays in Majorca were being advertised at £36 for eight days and £46 for fifteen days.
- In April a dance and cabaret was held in the Strathearn Hotel featuring Tony Morelli, Alex Matthews and the Professionals.
- Also in April, a new delicatessen opened in Orr's, offering such things as fresh mustard, Italian pasta and various curries.
- The John E. Meneely & Sons garage was offering 750 pink stamps or 20% cash discount for purchase of car tyres, and 45 stamps and glass vouchers on cash purchases of £1 or more on petrol.
- At a meeting of Holywood and Bangor councils in the Town Hall, it was agreed that they would henceforth operate as a single district council.
- A tender was accepted by the Urban District Council for the repair of copper roofing at the Queens Hall. There had only been one tender entered, at a cost of £124.35.

- The town surveyor applied to hire special plant to clean the Queens Hall dance floor. Around the same time a complaint had been received from a local woman's group about the state of the hall.
- As an aid to road safety and following a traffic survey by Holywood Council, it was proposed that the local parish priest be contacted regarding lowering the chapel wall at My Lady's Road and Belfast Road by about 2 feet and putting a railing on top to allow a better view for motorists. There had been quite a few near crashes at the spot.
- Romance was in the air when Holywood Library took advantage of an offer by a supplier to supply 100 volumes of romance novels at 40p each, less discount.
- Concerns were raised at a meeting of Holywood Urban District Council regarding cars parking on the footpaths at the Kinnegar. It was considered dangerous for pedestrians; especially as army lorries used the road on a regular basis. A suggestion was made to raise the height of the kerb but no action was taken on the matter.
- The Holywood through pass construction was well underway, and it was due to open in November.
- Holywood councillors discussed providing a public convenience at Redburn cemetery at a cost of around £200.

138

There had been numerous requests from members of the public about providing toilets.

- Creighton's Green reservoir contained 121 million gallons of water. There were 40 million gallons at the Holywood works.
- Holywood Further Education Centre ran an 18 week course in amateur small-boat building. This covered fitting out fiberglass hulls and the construction of dinghies.
- In December Councilor W. E. Russell asked the town surveyor to look at the signal box in Holywood railway station, which he described as looking like the Leaning Tower of Pisa. The town clerk was then to write to the railway company and inform them that it could well collapse. After investigating the matter, Northern Ireland Railways decided the structure was unsafe and as soon as re-signaling could be arranged (within four months) the old signal box would be demolished. In the meantime, a check would be kept on the building, the signal box was eventually demolished.
- Holywood Urban District Council was asked to investigate a complaint made by a local shopkeeper that a trader had been selling fish from a private car in the town.
- Down County Health Committee approached the Ministry with regard to purchasing property owned by the Belfast Savings Bank in Holywood, as it would round off the site for the health centre. A considerable amount of money was wanted for the property.

1972

- Some local businesses:
  Abbey National Building Society
  Arcadia Bakery
  D. Bamford, antiques
  Bell's Home Bakery
  Elliotts, confectioner
  Golden Hind, Chinese restaurant
  E. Herron, confectioner
  Kearney Bros., outfitters
  Kinnegar Service Station
  E. Allen, chemist

J. Ballagh & Sons
Belfast Co-Operative Society
The Railway Inn
J. Fogerty, newsagent
R. Henderson, auto engineers
Holywood Spar Stores
Kerwoods, housewear
Ladyneeds Ladies Outfitters

HOLYWOOD CRICKET CLUB

CHRISTMAS BAZAAR

Queen's Hall, Holywood : Friday, 1st Dec.

6.30 p.m. till 10.00 p.m.

Grocery, Cake, Fancy Goods Stalls and Tombola

FATHER CHRISTMAS AND SIDE SHOWS FOR THE CHILDREN

ADMISSION (Including Tea and Biscuits) · **1/6**

- Holywood through pass opened in 1972, stretching from the Palace Barracks through Marine Parade to Croft Road. The idea was to stop the congestion of traffic coming through Holywood, and a lot of business people believed this might mean a decline in business for Holywood town centre. Others took the opinion that it would mean less congestion and easier parking for motorists and customers. At a meeting of Holywood Council shortly after the opening, various complaints received about the speed of traffic on this new stretch were discussed.

- Petrol licenses were granted to some of the local garages at the time: Leslie Innis, J. B. Cowan, John Fox, J. E. Meneely & Son and the Priory Filling Station.

- Holidays in the sun were being advertised, such as 14 nights in Tenerife from £74, 14 nights on the Costa del Sol from £65 and 14 nights in Yugoslavia from £68.

- In April 'Miss Maxol', Jean Waddell, officially opened the Priory Self-Service Filling Station. This was a 24-hour   station,

and Green Shield stamps were handed out with purchases of petrol.
- Fashion wigs for men went on sale at the Wiggery in Holywood.
- There were four daily collections from Post Office pillar boxes.
- Some items for sale in local shops:

Toothpaste 10p
Fig rolls 5p
Vodka from £2.45
Whiskey from £2.68
New fridges from £34.90

- At Holywood Urban District Council, the future of Patton's Lane was under discussion. It was suggested that the Palace Bar, demolished by a bomb the previous year, might be developed as part of a major shopping precinct fronting onto the lane.
- In June 1972 Holywood town centre became a no-go area when barriers were set up to stop traffic due to a possible bomb threat. The High Street literally became a pedestrian zone, and other areas affected included part of Shore Road, part of Church Road and Hibernia Street.
- In December the first prosecution took place when a man was fined £20 for leaving his vehicle unattended in a control area. Police had been called to the unattended car, which had been parked for 50 minutes.
- Holywood Council warned bait diggers they were prepared to take legal action against anyone infringing the license obtained from the Board of Trade for commercial bait digging on the shore. Teams of diggers were coming from outside Holywood and digging on the shore. The police were notified.

47 HIGH STREET, HOLYWOOD

FOLK NIGHT
EVERY MONDAY THROUGH

MONDAY, 26th JANUARY

PINCH OF SNUFF

MONDAY, 2nd FEBRUARY

NATURAL FOLK

MONDAY, 9th FEBRUARY

BARMBRACK

Lounge open from 7 p.m. Music 9 – 11.15 p.m.
ADMISSION 75p

- Owners of unauthorized signs in the High Street were asked to remove them or apply for planning approval; more than 40 signs were involved.
- In February the *Spectator* newspaper celebrated its 23rd anniversary of coming to Holywood.

142

- Once again Holywood Council warned they would be taking legal proceedings against persons found infringing the bait-diggers' license. Despite repeated warnings, people were still coming from other towns to dig for bait.

- Entertainment licenses were granted for the following:
  Houston Hall
  Heasley Scout Hall
  Orange Hall
  High Street Presbyterian Church Hall
  Masonic Hall
  Fire Station
  Non-Subscribing Church Hall
  Old Parochial Hall
  St Patricks Hall
  Methodist Church
  Holywood Cinema
  Yacht Club
  Purple Star Social Club
  Secondary School
  Social Centre Loughview
  Girl Guide Hall, Sullivan Place
  Primary School
  Queens Hall
  Cricket Pavilion
  3rd Holywood Scout Group

- A grand charity show for the Combat Cancer campaign was held in the Queens Hall with James Young in a one man show. Admission was £1, and it included the chance for a lucky ticketholder to win a stereo record player.

- Holywood Urban District Council decided that no action would be taken for the time being on the engagement of traffic wardens.

- The Rev. Cannon Eric Barbour presented a Sunday service for the BBC, which was televised nationally directly from the church of St Philip and St James.

- At Kerwoods a 26 inch colour television could be rented for £1.95 a week. A 20 inch black-and–white television was 55p a week. Both came with three months' free viewing.

<u>1973</u>

- In June 1973 the new proprietors of the Strathearn Hotel intended to build an extension to the building.
- Kerwoods were selling Hoover spin dryers for £24, Tricity fridges for £36.95 and electric blankets for £4.75.
- John E. Meneely & Son were selling 1969 Morris 1100s for £625 and 1969 Morris 1800s for £795. They also offered an engine tune-up, plugs, ignition parts, condensers, air filters and rocket joints (BL Mini) for £268, 1971 Austin 1300 GTs for £850 and 1971 Morris 1100s for £750.

- Some television programmes:
  BBC 1:
  Pebble Mill
  Jackanory
  Blue Peter
  Scene Around Six
  Tomorrow's World
  Top of the Pops
  Mastermind

  BBC 2:
  Play School
  Opinion
  Real Time
  The Golden Bowl

  UTV:
  Romper Room
  General Hospital
  Crossroads

- Also in June, Holywood surveyor Mr F. Chestnutt, in his report to Holywood Urban District Council, reported that 5 million gallons of water had been used in the past week and that there were 70 million gallons in storage. This situation was worrying him. The council warned householders to try and conserve water. As a follow-up, in August there were 44 million gallons of water in storage and Mr Chestnutt warned that water restrictions may have to be brought in.
- E. A. Baird's had sunglasses on sale ranging from 14p to £19.80.
- Holywood Urban District Council requested that the sculptures of the late Rosamond Praeger be transferred to Holywood Public Library for permanent retention.
- Bangor Round Table held an all star wrestling match in the Queens Hall featuring Rasputin, The Mummy, Dave Finlay and Billy Joe Beck.

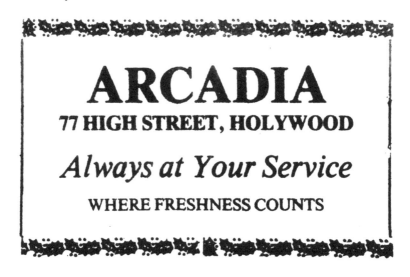

ARCADIA
77 HIGH STREET, HOLYWOOD

Always at Your Service

WHERE FRESHNESS COUNTS

- Some programmes on local television:

BBC 1:
Grandstand
The Virginian

UTV:
The Detectives
Scene Around Six

BBC 2:
Open University
Gardeners World
M*A*S*H
Open Door
Morecombe and Wise
Crossroads
Barnaby Jones
Police Six
Skippy
Sesame Street

- An inspection of the Queens Hall by the Fire Authority produced a long list of work required. This included things such as fire doors and a fire alarm system at the cost of £525.
- Plans were drawn up to turn Holywood town centre into a pedestrian precinct.

- Holywood Players presented 'Dirty Dick' in their second production of the season. This three-act production attracted a large audience and was a great success.
- Holywood traders held a meeting regarding the possibility of a proposed pedestrian precinct in the centre of the town. This was to include the High Street and parts of Shore Street and Church Road. It was decided to form a Traders Association who would then approach the local council.
- As part of their services to the community, Holywood Police sent out word around Holywood asking people if they had any fallen trees or knew of anyone who had run out of coal supplies. When some was found, off-duty Sergeant Lennox and Constable Merideth went along and sawed them up, and after bagging the wood presented it to those in need. The service was totally free. The Sergeant himself bought a trailer to transport the wood and local garages helped out with supplying a tow bar and petrol.
- Officers and men from the Royal Regiment of Wales after being contacted in the middle of a storm came to the rescue when a tree fell on the home of the Judge family. They arrived with equipment and tarpaulins to remove the wood and secure the roof.
- Some businesses operating at this time.

Stewarts Supermarket-The Tatler-Vanity Fair-
The Turntable-Shannons-Sheridans Confectionary
Redburn Garden Shop-McKimm Bros.-Lemons
Grainger Bros.-Isobel's Bakery-Kearney Brothers
Ladyneeds-Kingmac-Kinnegar C.&C.-Spar
John Ballagh-Belfast Co-Operative-Elliotts-
Golden Hind Chinese Restaurant

- In March it was proposed that traffic lights be erected at the junction of Redburn Square and the Holywood Bypass. In June the Department of the Environment stated that work would begin in early autumn.
- In May Holywood Rugby Union opened the new club grounds at Kerr Park.
- In February the Strathearn Hotel offered dancing with Marie Cunningham and Ray Kerr. An assortment of dancing styles was showcased, including the quickstep, foxtrot, waltz and cha-cha. There was a dinner dance cost of £3.00. A weekly cabaret also took place, with one of the artists being Joe E. Dee.

◊◊

HOLYWOOD AND DISTRICT COMMUNITY COUNCIL

FESTIVAL BALL
in The Queen's Hall, Holywood
Wednesday, 1st May, 1974

Dancing from 9 p.m.   Buffet Supper

TICKET £2.50

Application for tickets should be made before 29th March
to NOEL L. WILLIAMSON, 15 Ballymenoch Park, Holywood

Phone 2865 (Private) or 4510 (Business)

◆◆◆

1975

- The population of Holywood was around 7,980.
- Planning permission to convert St Valentine's on the Church Road into a hotel was turned down.
- In January Holywood Methodist Church was the target of vandals, and stained glass windows at the front and opposite Church View were damaged.

- Wm Stevenson & Sons' paint and wallpaper shop on the Church Road was selling woodchip paper at 49p a roll and embossed paper at £1 per roll.
- Holywood had the following societies and clubs:

  Golf Club
  Hockey Club
  Unionist Club
  Golden Age Club
  Trefoil Club
  Rugby Club
  Round Table
  Working Men's Club
  Women's Business & Professional Club
  Cricket and Lawn Tennis Club
  Horticultural Society
  Music Festival Association
  Over 60's Club
  Yacht Club
  Ladies' Bowling Society
  Players' Dramatic Society
  The Not Forgotten Association
- Holywood Cinema's license to show films was renewed by the council.
- Mary Peters officially opened St Colmcille's Youth Centre at Church View.
- North Down Borough Council authorized the redecoration of the Queens Hall at a cost of £1,100.
- In April leading fireman Tommy Catherwood received his Long Service and Good Conduct Medal from the Fire Authority. He had been in Holywood Fire Brigade for over 22 years.

WAGON WHEEL
COUNTRY CLUB at the
Strathern Hotel, Holywood
EVERY MONDAY, 9 p.m.—1 a.m.
MONDAY, 5th AUGUST
Sean Quinn & Down County
FRIDAY , 2nd AUGUST RODEO

- Some television programmes being shown:

BBC 1:
Lassie
Whatever Happened to the Likely Lads?
Jim'll Fix it
The Black and White Minstrel Show
Cannon
That's Life

BBC 2:
The Old Grey Whistle Test
Match of the Day
The World About Us
Open University
The Waltons

UTV:
World of Sport
New Faces
Sale of the Century
Sportsworld
Mad About the House

150

Holywood Urban District Council

WATER SHORTAGE

Owing to the reduced average rainfall over the past six years and constantly increasing usage, reserves of water in Holywood Reservoirs are being steadily depleted. The public are requested to note that **UNLESS SUPPLIES ARE CONSERVED NOW**, water rationing will be inevitable in the future.

Everyone is urged to prevent water wastage by having leaking appliances repaired, automatic flushing cisterns turned off when not in use and preventing loss by every other possible means.

THE USE OF WATER FOR WASHING CARS OR FOR WATERING GARDENS IS PROHIBITED UNTIL FURTHER NOTICE.

The co-operation of the general public in Holywood is now sought in an endeavour to safeguard our available reserves and thus prevent the introduction of more stringent restrictions within the next six weeks.

(BY ORDER)

1976

- In May a hosepipe ban came into force; it included Holywood and all of North Down. Garden watering and private car washing were banned. Water reserves in the Silent Valley were well below the level required and were giving cause for concern.

- May of this year also highlighted the opening of the new Transport Museum at Cultra. This had moved from Witham Street in Belfast, where it had been bursting at the seams with wonderful displays. Before its opening, people lined the railway banks to see two gigantic steam trains on their final journey to the museum. The museum was opened by the Duke of Abercorn with the RUC band providing music at the ceremony. This meant that the Transport Museum and the Folk Museum were situated side by side. From its opening in May until July, 18,200 people visited the museum.

Trains on the way to the Folk Museum

- The Strathearn Hotel started a Monday night disco with DJ David Hamilton. Admission was 50p. The disco was quite popular with locals.
- Kcarncy Bros. was advertising men's shoes from £3.50 and ladies' from £3.
- An accident happened at Sullivan Upper School when a gas cylinder exploded in a store room injuring two workmen. A fire started, which was extinguished by Holywood firemen.
- In November the famous maypole had to have a length cut off at the bottom due to traces of fungal decay. It had been erected in 1957. The pole was removed in order to carry out the work; it

was back in position in December, slightly shorter, but in better condition.
- Also in November, Holywood Fire Brigade was called to the Ulster Folk Museum when a water tank being installed caught fire whilst the fiberglass was being heated.
- Some television programmes we watched:

BBC 1:
Bewitched
Little House on the Prairie
Dr Who
Steptoe and Son
Kojak
Parkinson
It Ain't Half Hot Mum

BBC 2:
Open University
Play Away
Open Door
Network
The Money Programme

UTV:
Sesame Street
World of Sport
New Faces
The Protectors
Sale of the Century
General Hospital

LOOK INTO THE

HOLLYWOOD BOWL
HOLYWOOD

ON MONDAY NIGHT

when mine hosts

JACK HILL AND MARSHALL SHEARER

would like to welcome old and new customers alike

THE HOLLYWOOD BOWL
HIGH STREET, HOLYWOOD

YOUR OLD AND NEW LOCAL

- In February Jack and Jill, the cats from BBC's *Blue Peter*, were a big attraction at the Queens Hall. This was in aid of the Northern Ireland Cat Club Show, in which cats from blue Burmese to tailless Manx were on show.
- John E. Meneely & Sons garage were offering 80 Green Shield stamps and a glass voucher with every purchase of £2.00 worth of petrol.
- On 9th February Redburn Cabaret Lounge, situated off the Old Holywood Road, opened its doors. (It's now a nursing home.) The resident compère was Billy Byers and admission was 75p. The gala night also featured guest artistes Young Winston, Billy Roberts and Crystal Clark.
- A brand new Skoda could be bought from local garages for £1,345.

154

- After a sponsored disco involving the Blue Lamp Disco, Holywood Youth Council raised enough money to purchase a new minibus.

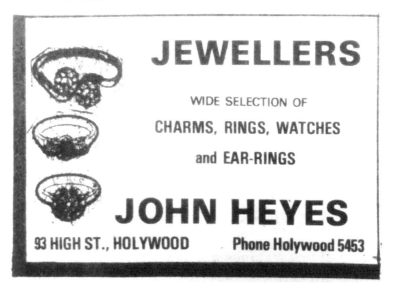

JEWELLERS

WIDE SELECTION OF

CHARMS, RINGS, WATCHES

and EAR-RINGS

JOHN HEYES

93 HIGH ST., HOLYWOOD   Phone Holywood 5453

1977

- Some local businesses:

H. S. Warwick
Ladyneeds Children's Clothes
J. Heyes, jeweller
The Carpet Shop
Norwood Pharmacy
Pepper Mill Restaurant
Home Décor
Ted's Fruit & Veg
Regency Insurance
Down Office Equipment
Isobel's Home Bakery
Vanity Fair
Sport & Leisure

Wilson Shoes
Kinnegar Service Station
Maypole Radio & Television
Hanna's Flowers
Holywood Glazing Contractors
Sweeny's Pharmacy
Kinnegar Cash Stores
Kerwoods, hardware
Holywood DIY
Mod-Elle Fashions
Holywood Wine Market
Terence McKeag Cars
Tog's Ices
E. Herron, sweets and cigarettes
Art & Home
The Wool Sack
Bells Bakery
Norwood Pharmacy
Kearney Bros., outfitters
Holywood Fruit Market
J. E. Meneely, garage
Shannon's Newsagents
The Schooner Restaurant
The Coffee House
Executive Travel
William Moffett & Son, butchers
Holywood Frozen Food Centre

- Local garage John E. Meneely was selling tyres at the following prices:
  - Tubeless (remoulds): £5.10 (crossply); £7.10 (radial)
  - Tubeless (new): £8.75 (crossply); £9.00 (radial)
- For Jazz lovers, George Chisholm appeared in the Apex Jazz Band in the Queens Hall. Admission was £1.50.
- Seapark PHAB (Physically Handicapped and Able Bodied) Club held a cabaret and dance in the Strathearn Hotel. Admission was £1.

- Some television programmes being shown in 1977:

BBC 1:
Grandstand
Jim'll Fix It
Dr Who
Parkinson
Holiday
That's Life
Starsky and Hutch
University Challenge
BBC 2:
Play Away
Horizon
Mr Magoo
The Lively Arts
Dastardly & Muttley
Open to Question
ITV:
Merrie Melodies
Sesame Street
The Bionic Woman
The Muppet Show
New Faces
Stars on Sunday

HOLYWOOD CHAMBER OF TRADE
(On behalf of Holywood Community Council)
invite you to the

COMMUNITY BALL

in the

QUEEN'S HALL, HOLYWOOD
ON WEDNESDAY, 30th APRIL

Dancing 9—2 a.m. to the

PHOENIX SHOWBAND

+ CABARET   + TOMBOLA
+ SUPPER   + MAY QUEEN CROWNING
+ BAR   + DRESS OPTIONAL

TICKETS £2.75 each

Available from E. Herron & Son 20-22 Church Road
P. Lavery, 79 High Street, K. Zalenka, 153 High Street

Tables bookable in advance

- Among some of the cars for sale by well-known Holywood man George Kilby at Kinnegar Service Station were:
  - 1969 Ford Cortina 1600E, gold (£250)
  - 1973 Toyota Celica, metallic blue (£1,495)
  - 1972 Datsun Coupe 1200, red (£795)
  - 1969 Vauxhall Viva, green, two doors (£265)
- To mark the Queen's Silver Jubilee, a grand fireworks display was held on Monday 6th June at Seapark. On 9th June Music for the Jubilee was held at the church of St Philip and St James. Music was provided by Brian Hunter LGSM and the church choir.

- Culloden Country Club held, in the Culloden Hotel, its first 'live' Downtown Radio transmission of The Big T show.
- An oven-ready roasting chicken could be bought at Moffett's, the butcher on Downshire Road, for £1.20.
- North Down Borough Council's Services Committee discussed remedial work to be carried out at the Kinnegar sea wall. The estimated cost would be in the region of £25,750, so it was decided to put the job out to tender.

HOLYWOOD THEN & NOW
EXHIBITION

1978

- An exhibition was held in the Queens Hall entitled 'Holywood Then and Now'. It involved around 49 exhibitors looking back at Holywood's past and considering how it compared to the present day. There were local schools, churches, football and cricket clubs, golf clubs, Peace People, the Royal British Legion and the Mothers' Union, among others.
- The 3rd Holywood Scouts celebrated their 35th Anniversary with a buffet supper and birthday cake.
- Holywood Tyre & Battery opened new premises formerly used by Terence McKeag who used it as a showroom.
- In February a Croft Road resident got the shock of her life when looking out the kitchen window. A huge lorry came ploughing through her hedge luckily coming to a stop in the garden in front of her. It had been left on a hill with the engine running. No one was injured.

- Some television programmes being watched in 1978:

BBC 1:
Open University
The Flashing Blade
Network
Dad's Army
The Mill
Record Breakers
Grandstand
The Val Doonican Show

BBC 2:
The Money Programme
M*A*S*H
Network
Horizon
A Bird's Life
Planets

ITV:
Sesame Street
Celebrity Squares
Sale of the Century
Police Woman
The Muppet Show
World of Sport
South Bank Show
Horse Trials

A car on fire in High Street (Photo: Courtesy of the County Down Spectator)

- The Ulster Bank in Holywood was the only local bank that had what was then called a Unique Cash Dispenser Unit (now known as an ATM) for withdrawing cash.
- Flooding brought chaos to the Kinnegar after 24 hours of rain. Water was right up to the entrance of the Ordnance Depot.
- Holywood residents were able to view draft plans that set out the proposals for the town up until 1991. This included the stop line or border with Belfast, Greenfield sites, older houses with a view to development of the land they were on, employment, shopping, recreation and the health service, among other things.
- In April work began on the first phase of the Queens Hall Community Centre scheme.
- Also in April, the Heasley Hall headquarters of 1st Holywood Scout Troop was officially opened following extensive renovations. The service was carried out by Mrs J. McCaw, daughter of Mr Heasley after whom the hall was named. Cost of the work came to £12,900.
- Holywood Social and Recreation Club held a talent contest with a prize of £500.

- The Ulster Orchestra held a summer prom in the Queens Hall. Admission was £1.
- The Holywood Players carried out a household survey to discover potential attitudes towards local amateur drama. The survey covered 500 households.
- The local fire brigade were called to a fire at the Unit Construction Company. Some wooden materials were destroyed. The cause of the fire was unknown.
- Fold Housing Association obtained planning permission to erect an old people's dwelling on the site known as 'Spafield'. However, the historical buildings branch of the Department of The Environment had not decided whether to allow demolition of the existing dormant Georgian building.
- In December, 30 former members of the original children's choir who sang at the Holywood maypole 30 years before sang carols outside the First Holywood Non-subscribing Church.
- At a meeting of Holywood District Horticultural Society the Society decided to change their name to Holywood Gardening Society.
- In September Holywood and Knock fire brigades were called to St Valentine's, a house on the Church Road. The top floor was badly burnt and it took firemen four hours to bring the fire under control. The fire was spotted and reported by a pilot of a Short Skyvan who was flying over the town at the time.
- A Holywood man appeared at the local magistrate's court on a charge of stealing two hens. The hens were valued at £1.50.

St. Valentines

<u>1979</u>

- Some local businesses:

Bells' Bakery
John Cairnduff, builder
The Tatler Newsagent
Baird Chemist
Down Office Equipment
Unit Construction
Spar Store
Stewarts Supermarket
The Peppermill Restaurant
The Turntable
Holywood Taxis
P. Lavery, chemist
The Wool Shop

Clarke Car Care
Brown Funeral Furnishers
John Hayes, jeweller
Martello Inn
The Railway Inn
The Hob
R. Richards, electrical
The Seahorse Inn
Kingmac Cash & Carry
The Schooner Restaurant
Shannon's Newsagents
J. Jennings, greengrocer
Wm Stevenson & Sons
Lions Maid Ice Cream

- For those who enjoyed folk music, the Martello Inn on the High Street was the place to go. They had regular groups such as the Pikemen playing.
- In January flooding at the Kinnegar was highlighted again when some of the sea wall defences collapsed, increasing flooding in the area. The Department of Environment said that the situation was under review and they were seeking a solution. Many houses were flooded, destroying carpets, furniture, etc. and some houses had up to 18 inches of water on the ground floor! Short-term measures were put in place, which included supplying sand bags. The shore wall eventually had large boulders placed along the beach to try and break up the incoming waves. Holywood Residents Association had a meeting with North Down Council regarding the flooding and eventually a contract for repair to the sea wall was put out to tender. The tender was awarded, and work was to begin in November.
- The clock in the Old Priory finally returned to working order after a break of nearly 12 months. Time stood still no more.
- Mr John Frost, headmaster of Sullivan Upper School, broke the news that he was to retire in June.

164

- Holywood Players had a great success with *Big Bad Mouse*, which was performed over a period of three evenings.
- In November the new St Patrick's Hall was opened in Church View.
- A fuel drivers' strike led to the closure of some schools. Holywood High School and St Patrick's had to close their doors due to a lack of heating as fuel ran out.
- In September the famous Acker Bilk and the Paramount Jazz Band played at the Culloden Hotel. One of Acker's most famous hits was 'Stranger on the Shore'.
- A television license at this time cost £34.

Clanbrassil House, Cultra

invite you to visit them for

SPECIAL BUFFET

on

EASTER MONDAY and TUESDAY
3rd and 4th APRIL

FULL INCLUSIVE PRICE £1.25
from 12 noon till 10 p.m.

Book early to avoid disappointment

Telephone HOLYWOOD 3147

1981

- Holywood businessman Terence McKeag became the new president of Holywood Club of Trade.
- Holywood Cricket Club celebrated its centenary and produced a brochure recording its history. A reception and dance was held, which was attended by the president and secretary of the Irish Cricket Union from Dublin as well as other distinguished guests.
- Saltwater Brigg provided entertainment in Chiccarinos.

166

- Holywood Yacht Club was granted the use of additional land at the Esplanade/Kinnegar Road for the purpose of extending the existing dingy park. North Down Borough Council agreed to grant a 99 year lease on payment of £85 for the use of the original smaller area from 1973. The ground rent was to be reviewed every five years.

1982

- A number of complaints were received at Holywood Residents Association regarding people on horses using the foreshore footpath between Kinnegar railway arch and Seapark.
- John E. Meneely was selling the new Morris Ital, prices started at £3,900.
- Holywood and district Combat Cancer Group organized a successful sponsored roller disco in the town's Roller Disco based in the old Holywood Cinema.
- Holywood had a gym club with over 70 members aspiring to become gymnasts.
- Kerwoods were selling black-and-white portable televisions for £35 and colour portables for £199.
- In 2010, during excavation work by NIE, human remains were discovered by workmen beside the Old Priory Church and its graveyard. Forensics experts and police were called to investigate but, after examination, it was believed that the bones were possibly up to several hundred years old. It was concluded that the bones were probably from what was part of the original cemetery, which may have extended beyond the existing one.

Scene of the bones find

- Over 400 young people attended the annual St George's Day parade in Holywood. This involved the Beavers, Scouts, Cubs, Bunnies, Brownies and Guides. The parade was led by the North Irish Horse to the grounds of St Philip and St James.
- The Sacred Heart of Mary Grammar School, Holywood, presented £3,146 to Action Research for the Crippled Child. They raised the money through a sponsored dance and street collections.
- In May the Holywood Rudolf Steiner School opened a new craft and science block. The block was converted from an old outhouse, much of the work being done by parents and teachers.
- Holywood Frozen Food Centre was selling 10 inch pizzas for 90p.
- North Down Borough Council asked the Department of the Environment Water Service to investigate complaints about the quality of the Holywood water supply at certain times of the day. It was thought that chemicals in the water may be affecting it. The affected areas were Church Road, Spencer Street and Trevor Street.

168

Mister Softee ice cream vehicle

1984

- Built in 1862, work was in progress to save the old Sullivan School building in the High Street from dry rot, pigeons and deterioration after lying empty. The circular staircase had to be ripped out because of decay. North Down Borough Council discussed various uses for the building. The building eventually became Holywood Library.
- Leisure Kerr Ltd Travel of Holywood was offering holidays to Spain for £229 for two weeks inclusive.
- In May Glenlyon River Park on the Church Road was opened, boasting a river, picnic facilities, viewing platforms and a network of walking paths.
- A malicious fire at Holywood Golf Club caused scorch marks and damage to curtains.
- In November Priory Filling Station had a free Christmas Draw for two turkeys each week until Christmas.

HOW THINGS HAVE CHANGED

(Some of the author's personal memories)

- A refuse collector of today would cringe at the job that a bin man (as he was known years ago) had to do. All our bins were made of metal with a metal lid. Collections were done once a week with everything thrown into one bin, unlike today. In Holywood, when your bin man came along he had to walk around to the rear of your premises, lift and carry the bin *on his back* to the front of the premises to be emptied. After he tipped the contents into the bin lorry he then had to carry the empty bin and place it back where he found it. All the property owner had to do was fill the bin... changed days.

- Black-faced from coal dust, coalmen with a lorry full of coal sacks were also a common sight, carrying bags of coal from their lorries on their backs and delivering them to people's houses.

- In addition to selling petrol, all the garages that used to be in Holywood carried out mechanical work to your car if required, such as servicing. Each one was owned by a mechanic or had mechanics working for them, and they fixed punctures, checked your oil, adjusted your points, etc.

- There was once a postal delivery service three times a day; this was good for businesses that were perhaps waiting for a cheque to be delivered.

- Before the Holywood bypass was created, Redburn Square was basically that: a square. Vehicle traffic was not a big issue, the bulk being buses or vehicles arriving at or departing from the railway station to drop or pick up passengers or parcels. When walking in that direction, at Sullivan Place you passed the fire station – the original was situated beside the Town Hall; Electric Board office, where you could pay bills or buy appliances; Masonic Hall; King Edward VII Memorial Hall; Girl Guides' Hall; Orange Hall (which was used as a courthouse); Grainger's; and the Queens Hall. The Queens Hall was used as council offices, and at that time Holywood had their own councilors who dealt with local matters. As well as

170

the railway station, the square also housed the bus station and the Mr Softee Ice Cream Depot. The soldiers' statue stood near the middle of the square and a red phone box stood outside the Orange Hall. At the other side of the square was Marine Parade, two rows of very large, majestic houses facing each other; one row was eventually knocked down to cater for the bypass. Another road led up past what was Rosamond Praeger's art studio and onto the High Street. There were usually some buses parked in the square and Mr Softee vans could be seen going to and fro on a regular basis. The train station was usually quite busy with vehicles and pedestrians either catching or coming from a train. Eventually the square was to be cut up by the new bypass, opening it up to a never-ending flow of traffic.

The railway station was covered. As you walked through it, past the ticket office, you came to a little shop nestled in the corner selling cigarettes, tobacco, sweets, etc. This then led up to the Belfast platform, and a subway under the railway line brought you to the Bangor platform on the other side of the track. Here stood a large signal box, which eventually had to be demolished, and in the background you could see the old Holywood gasworks and large gas storage tanks. The subway which ran underneath the railway track and allowed you to walk through to the platform for Bangor or the seashore ran at a bit of a slope, and kids loved running up and down it yelling, as it had a great echo effect, much to the dismay of the stationmaster! The tunnel may well still exist, perhaps having been simply blocked up at both ends. The goods yard at the rear of the station eventually became the bus depot.

- Today's children are inundated with a variety of toys and electronic entertainment to keep them occupied, including computers, MP3s, DVDs, iPads mobile phones, portable games, and so on – all items that can produce endless entertainment at the flick of a switch. Entertainment years ago was limited to simpler options. After-school football was a favorite outdoor sport if the weather was fine; all you needed was a ball. This could mean playing on what was known as Barney's Field or, as traffic wasn't as bad then as it is now, a street became a football pitch with jackets or jumpers becoming the goal posts. Another game played (which some children might still play now when they are not playing with their computer) was cowboys and Indians, careering up and down the street or alleyways with pieces of wood replicating a gun. If you didn't have any wood, your fingers became a revolver, and if you had been given a toy gun for your birthday it was even better, providing authentic sound effects with rolls of caps. Skipping with a rope was another way to entertain yourself, as was conkers, hide and seek, hopscotch and hoop and cleek, which involved running along with a bicycle wheel minus the tyre and a long piece of metal to keep the wheel rolling whilst you guided it. If you had the wheels, axles and some wood you could put together a cart

172

and ride it down a hill. The problem came when you got to the bottom if you had not built some sort of braking system! Marbles was another favorite game, swapping coloured balls of glass that we thought would be a winner in every game. One flick of the thumb meant the difference between winner and loser; technology had not taken off yet so games were simple for boys and girls. As years went on and parents could afford them, other toys became popular, such as Scalectrix, Meccano and GI Joe for boys; girls loved things like Barbie dolls, prams and kitchen sets. In the 1960s and 1970s, one of the 'in' things for teenagers to have (in addition to a record player) was a transistor radio, it was portable and could be tuned into stations like Radio Caroline to capture all the latest pop music.

- Pre-decimal money used at the time included coins such as: pennies, halfpennies, sixpences, threepenny pieces, one shilling, two shillings, half crowns, farthings. Paper notes consisted of ten shillings, one pound, five pound and ten pound. There were no ATM machines but quite a few banks as they were the only places where you could withdraw money.

- The telegram was the fastest way to send a message if you had no telephone, delivered by a boy on a bicycle or small motorbike.

- Cameras were very basic, a popular one being the Kodak Brownie for taking family photographs. A lot of cameras used flash cubes for indoors or to illuminate dark areas. These sometimes came in the form of a small cube with about four flashbulbs in it. When one bulb was used you then turned the cube around, which meant a new bulb ready for use. Other cameras had single bulbs which, when used, were taken out and replaced. Rolls of film were used to capture the pictures; black-and-white photographs were the norm until colour came along (or until you could afford colour film). Eventually film was produced in a cartridge. Cine cameras were around but more expensive.

- Holywood Youth Club was started to give the younger people of Holywood somewhere to go and to keep them off the streets.

173

This proved quite popular and provided various activities for the young.

- At one time Muffin the Mule, a favorite television star puppet, paid a visit to the Queens Hall much to the enjoyment of Holywood's youth. A show was put on with Muffin and other favorite characters such as Louise the Lamb and Grace the Giraffe.

- Some favorite shops in Holywood were Elliotts, the Arcadia, Bell's Bakery and Tog's Ices, probably because these were where we would all go to buy ice cream, sweets or buns when we could afford them.

- For some years the circus would come to town. Their large tent was erected in what is now the car park nearly opposite My Lady's Mile. As youngsters, this was a time to explore and peep into the various cages, hoping not to meet a lion! Some would try to crawl under the edge of the big-top tent and see the show for free, only to be put out by a member of the circus staff. A funfair on occasions also used the same location to set up their dodgem cars, merry-go-round and swing chairs, along with various stalls. In the evening, in the flashing coloured lights, it was fascinating to watch everyone screaming, shouting and enjoying themselves as they bumped into each other on the dodgems or held on to their seats as they hurtled around on the swing chairs.

- Years ago, Holywood firemen were called to a fire by a wailing siren situated on the fire station roof. There were no bleepers then, so this alert could be heard throughout the town unless the wind was blowing in the wrong direction. As the engine left the fire station there were no two-tone horns or blue flashing lights, just a fireman pulling on a plaited rope that was attached to a bell on the roof. In later years this changed to two automatic bells on the roof and two orange flashing lights on the front of the tender. Another vehicle which sat in the station for some years was what was known to people as a Green Goddess fire engine; this was used by the civil defense.

- Around the 1960s one sight in Holywood each week would be a horse and cart slowly making its way through the streets with the driver shouting, 'Coal brick; coal brick.' These were small blocks of what would probably have been compressed coal dust, a cheap alternative to coal. As the coal brick had recently been made, steam could be seen rising from the cart as the driver made his rounds. The blocks burnt quite slowly on a fire and gave out a good heat.

- Tog's ice cream shop on the High Street was a favorite location on any day, winter or summer. Outside the shop stood a large plastic ice cream cone which was like a homing beacon to everyone passing by. Inside the shop you could buy delicious sliders, cones, ice lollies, and 99s.

The Wiggery

SEE THE LATEST

Wigs and Hairpieces

115 HIGH STREET

HOLYWOOD

Phone: 3193

- Before the Holywood bypass most cars heading to Bangor had to come along the High Street, which led to more customers for Tog's, especially on a hot day. But no matter what the weather or season, there was usually a queue of adults and smiling kids at the counter buying the delicious homemade ice cream. You could have it with bananas, mixed fruit, lemonade, wafers, or just on its own. An ice cream soda was a great treat for visitors – this consisted of a large dab of ice cream in a tall glass mixed with lemonade and served with a long spoon. Upstairs was a small café, divided into cubicles, which served a variety of hot and cold drinks as well as ice cream. This was a favourite haunt for the younger generation, and the same faces could be seen there on a regular basis – at the time it was the 'in' place to be. Upon receipt of a coin, the jukebox played all the latest vinyl records. Tog's produced their own chocolate Easter eggs which were sold in many shops around the country.

- Before diesel trains came along steam trains were a regular sight, puffing their way to and from Belfast and Bangor every day. As well as from their billowing smoke, they were sometimes noticeable because of the fires they started on the embankment: on a dry day sparks and hot ashes would set the grass on fire! Holywood had its own gas tanks and gas was stored not too far from the railway line and station, so this could be a worrying time because of the potential for gas leakage. All along the side of the track burnt-out patches of grass could be seen.

- There have been a number of popular restaurants in Holywood over the years, and two that were quite popular were the Peppermill and the Schooner. Although perhaps classed as more expensive at the time, they produced a great variety of good food.

- The Automobile Association staff could be seen in their brown uniforms travelling through Holywood on their motorcycles with sidecar. They would also call into the local garages and update the owners on any new regulations. Members wore an AA metal badge on their cars. Upon seeing this, the AA patrolman would salute as the driver passed him by, if there was a police speed trap in the area the patrolman would not salute. Also dotted around the countryside were the familiar yellow-and-black AA telephone boxes that could be used by members in emergencies; inside each of these boxes was a telephone, various maps and contact information. Joining the AA got you a key for access to the boxes.

- For quite a while, on a Saturday night the Queens Hall became the focal point for the young people of Holywood and visitors from Belfast. Regular dances were held, with 'big band' groups providing the sounds as dancers gyrated to the music. Many romances started and finished here as dancers danced the night away, meeting new girlfriends and boyfriends.

- In 1979 St Colmcille's Youth Club became the talk of Holywood when stories emerged of it being haunted. Strange noises were heard on a number of occasions; despite the premises, including the roof space, being searched nothing was found, but the noises persisted. Whether the noises were from some natural phenomena no one knew, but they disappeared with time.

- You looked forward to getting a new pair of shoes in Kearney Bros., where there was what appeared to be a space-age machine that X-rayed your feet. When you tried on your shoes, you stepped into the machine and looked down into a screen where you could see your feet inside your new shoes. It was possible then to see if they fitted your feet properly. As youngsters, this appeared to be like something out of a Flash Gordon movie. Kearney Bros. also had a wonderful piping system throughout the building to transfer money or paperwork. When a canister of money was put into it you heard a loud sucking noise as the container was drawn through it to its destination.

- The 1960s were the days of Mods and Rockers, and whilst travelling around Holywood you could see a variety of people who followed either trend. The rockers were wearing all leather gear and riding motorbikes whilst the more moderate Mods rode around on scooters. Although each group had their different beliefs and opinions and appeared militant to the other, when in Tog's you could see them chatting away like good friends, usually with an ice cream in their hand. For a time, miniskirts became fashionable for women whilst men wore flared trousers. Favorite music stars were, The Beatles, The Rolling Stones, Elvis, Cliff Richard and The Shadows.

- One day we youngsters all looked in amazement at a car that was parked outside Kearney Bros. It was an Amphicar, which could go into water like a boat, and we peered underneath in awe at the sight of a large propeller! We waited around to see if the owner was going to drive to the Kinnegar and set sail, or sink. None of us could figure out where the lifejackets were kept.

- Years ago in Holywood, there seemed to be a great amount of snow every year, much to our delight; everyone headed to the golf links with all sorts of makeshift sleighs. Holywood Golf Course became a Mecca for tobogganing, and all you could see by moonlight on the snow-covered grass was various bodies wrapped up in scarves, gloves and wellie boots, plummeting down the hill on sleighs or improvised bits of cardboard and plastic.

- Some people used to love it when the roads were being re-tarred; they loved the smell of the new tar, but even more so the wonderful sight of the great, powerful steamroller. This massive metal beast of a machine had great billows of smoke and steam bursting out of its chimney as it rattled backwards and forwards, its massive weight flattening the tar.
- Any time there was a hard frost or ice, all our roads including the side roads and footpaths were gritted – this unfortunately is no longer the case.
- Every morning, when bleary eyed, your ears pricked up to the sound of glass bottles clinking as the early morning milkman went about his business, delivering fresh milk around the doorsteps and collecting the old bottles. Peering out in the darkness, you could see him and his helper weaving in and out of each house and hear the sound of the milk cart as it slowly made its way along the road.
- Another familiar sight was the fish merchant with an open-backed lorry full of fish for sale. The fish were always interesting to look at and touch but had quite a fishy smell – you avoided them touching your clothes!
- At the corner of the Old Priory there stood for many years a large horse trough where a horse could stop and have a refreshing drink of water. This was about the size of a bath and, although today it would be appreciated as a tourist attraction, for some unknown reason it was removed. I believe it was offered to the Ulster Folk Museum.
- Red telephone boxes with their numerous little panes of glass were a common sight around the town. Mobile phones were in their absolute infancy and had yet to make an impact. To make a call you inserted your money, dialed the number then, when connected, pressed button A. If it was the wrong number, button B was pressed to retrieve your money. Telephone boxes evolved along with the technological changes in phones, until eventually the red phone box with its many panes of glass disappeared, replaced with more modern versions.
- When there were no computers to type out a letter a mechanical or electronic typewriter was used. Perhaps looked upon today as

a cumbersome piece of equipment it was vital for typing out documents and letters. Using ones fingers you had to push hard on the letter keys to ensure it hit the ink ribbon hard enough to produce an impression on the paper. As there were no photocopiers a sheet of carbon paper was placed between two sheets if you wanted a copy made out. No spell checker then.

- In 1968 plans were drawn up to start a hovercraft cross-channel service operating from Holywood to Scotland and England. The hover terminal would have been based at the Kinnegar with rail links to Belfast, but unfortunately it never materialized.

I hope you enjoyed reminiscing on some snippets of Holywood's past. People and buildings make up a town or village and give it its character. Holywood has its share of both, and they are all (and have all been) unique to the town. Older people will remember the good times, the bad times and the changes, but no matter where they go, in their hearts Holywood will always be their town.